The Passion With-In

Interviews, testimonies, real life stories from passionate people, and much more…

Passion With-in
Printed in the United States of America
By O hill Publishing

Giving Back 365 days a year
A portion of the proceeds (10%) of all sales of this book and all books produced from this author will be donated to churches, nonprofit organizations in Maryland to improve education, domestic violence, health, human and civil rights, and sexual awareness. For more information, contact the author via inspiredsome1@gmail.com

Copyright © 2014 by Oumar J Hill
All rights reserved. No part of this book may be used or reproduced in any manner whatsoever without written permission, except in the case of brief quotations embodied in critical articles and reviews. This Book is licensed for personal enjoyment only. This Book may not be resold or given away to other people. If you would like to share this book with another person, please purchase an additional copy for each recipient.

Disclaimer and Legal Notices
The information presented in this book represents the view of the author as of the date of publication. This view is based upon research and personal experience. The author expressly reserves the right to alter and update his opinion in the future if conditions and circumstances so warrant. The material contained herein is general advice only and should not substitute for professional medical or psychological advice. Wherever necessary, please seek guidance from an accredited specialist before implementing tips that affect your body and mind.

OTHER
MOTIVATIONAL, EDUCATIONAL AND INSPIRING BOOKS
BY OUMAR HILL

- ✓ **Passion With-in workbook (Recommended read)**
- ✓ **Mastering Your Craft**
- ✓ **How to love yourself 1st in 14days**
- ✓ **How to love yourself 1st workbook week 1**
- ✓ **How to love yourself 1st workbook week 2**

In addition to the books above, visit the author on www.passionwith-in.com to share your testimony, read passion blog, provide your point of view, or to just gain inspiration.

The Passion With-In

OUMAR J. HILL

O. HILL & ASSOCIATES

CONTENTS

INTRODUCTION
Focus of the book — 10
Goals — 12
Passion is Everything — 14
No to Violence — 17
Starts at Home — 20
Interview: *Domestic Violence Survivor* — 22

SECTION I: DISCOVERY

CHAPTER 1: DIG DEEPER
Dive into you — 30
Dreams are real — 31
When I grow up? — 32
Passion perspective — 36
Passion Zone — 38
Multiple Passion-itis — 39
Positive & Negative Passion — 41
Change Negative to Positive — 42
Purpose — 43
Get up — 44

CHAPTER 2: FIND IT WITH IN
Find it — 49
Understand we are enough — 50
Pursue Happiness — 54
Manage Life — 59
Do Better — 63
Failure is not an option — 67

SECTION II: FUEL

CHAPTER 3: MAXIMIZING PASSION

TESTIMONY: *SEXUAL ASSAULT SURVIVOR*	73
ACCEPTING ADVERSITY	74
PASSION MAYBE UNCOMFORTABLE	76
FIGHTING FIRE WITH WATER	78
TURNING FEAR INTO STRENGTH	79
ASSOCIATE WITH WHO YOU WANT TO BECOME	81
MANAGE DISTRACTIONS	83

CHAPTER 4: KEY FACTORS WITHIN YOU

AMBITION	88
HONESTY	89
PATIENCE	90
FAITH	91
SELF-LOVE	92
FOCUS	94
HAVE INTANGIBLE SKILLS	95
SELF-EDUCATION	97
TESTIMONY: *10 TUMORS & NO EXCUSES, TO LEADERSHIP.*	98
BE YOURSELF	101
PRO BONO	102

SECTION III UNIQUENESS

CHAPTER 5: PASSIONPRENUERS

WHAT IS A PASSIONPRENEUR	106
SETBACKS = SETUPS	108
SUPERSTARS NEVER QUIT	108
BENEFITS OF FOLLOWING OUR PASSION	113

CHAPTER 6: PASSIONPRENUER SURVEY RESPONSE

JOURNALIST, JOHANNESBURG, SA	120

POET, NEW YORK, US	124
LIFE COACH, CONNECTICUT, US	127
PHILANTHROPIST, SOUTH CAROLINA, US	133
ENTREPRENEUR, CHICAGO, US	136
COMMUNITY ACTIVIST, WASHINGTON DC, US	140
MILITARY MOM, VIRGINIA, US	145

CHAPTER 7: BE COMPASSIONATE

TESTIMONY: *TRUE LOVE SEES NO FAULT*	150
ADD COMPASSION	151
COMPASSION STEPS	152
COMPASSIONEERS	156
TESTIMONY: *TAKES A VILLAGE*	156
INTERVIEW: *PASSION OVER MURDER*	158
PASSION OVER 9/11	162
PASSION OVER STRESS	163

SECTION IV: MENTAL PERSPECTIVE

CHAPTER 8: MIND OVER MATTER

MASLOW'S HIERARCHY OF NEEDS	166
CHARACTERISTICS OF SELF-ACTUALIZED PEOPLE	169
PASSION PYRAMID	172

CHAPTER 9: PASSION LIFE CYCLE

BIRTH	181
PURSUIT	181
NEGATIVE FEEDBACK	182
PASSION ANGELS & FRUITS	184
PASSION ZONE	189
PERFECTING PASSION	190
GET PAID FOR YOUR PASSION	191
FIND YOUR PURPOSE	193

HELP SOMEONE FIND THEIR PASSION	194

SECTION V: AUTHORS'S TESTIMONY

CHAPTER 10: AUTHOR'S PASSION STORIES

PART 1- MOTHER'S STRENGTH	196
ARRIVING AT THE HOSPITAL	197
POST-SURGERY	198
ROAD TO RECOVERY	199
COACHING AND MENTORING	200
SELF-DISCOVERY	202
ACCEPTANCE	204
SHARE YOUR STORY	209
ACKNOWLEDGEMENT	210
ABOUT AUTHOR	212

NOTES   213

-INTRODUCTION-
Basis of the book…..

"I am going to leave this world someday, so maybe I should leave the world with the gift of my passion"
-Oumar Hill

FOCUS OF BOOK

When life knocks us down we must look up into the sky and imagine ourselves up in the air, looking up at our feet dangling beneath us and forget about the troubles, which knocked us on our feet. Then when we arise with the passion and purpose to fly, we will with flying colors.

The focus of this book is to teach the world about the art of passion and the secrets behind the art. The world we dwell in is full of successful people who did not stop pursuing their dreams for whatever reason; however, there are more people who decided not to continue following their dreams. We will take a look at both sides of the pendulum and help those who quit get back on the right path, and those who have found their passion stay on the straight and narrow.

A set back is actually a step up only if we change our perspective on the events and think with purposeful intentions.

While attending college, an older friend of mine was going through a divorce and had to reconstruct her life from the ground up She had nothing externally or internally. Her first question was, "Where do I start, how do I just get up?" I don't know her spouse personally (there is always three side to a story – his, hers, and the truth), but I had to provide her with some comfort, common sense and constructive feedback to help her find her way. I imagined what my mother thought about when she experienced divorce with my dad. I called her asking, "How did you get up?" Dumbfounded at first, my mother clearly stated, and "What other choice do I have? I can either get up or get left behind. Something inside me told me to keep going on and do it with love and kindness".

The "passion within" is not only about the things we want

to do for a living, but the things that help us get over the humps in our life and help us to move forward with our head high and spirit full of confidence. In Chapter Eleven I will share how my mother used prayer, love, acceptance, patience, and forgiveness to fight her ordeal with cancer and how she recovered. She has always been and will continue to be my solid foundation full of recommendations and discipline. Without her love and guidance, I would have never become the person I am today.

This book was constructed with the intent to not only infuse people with energy to pursue their passion, but also to give people confidence, whom have been bullied, depressed, attacked, divorced and just looking for self-love. This book is a living document, which will live with us forever and help us throughout our life create, find and manage our passion. The book has been divided into the following sections, which have multiple chapters within them:

1. **Introduction**-*Background on the book and interview with married mom who survived domestic violence*
2. **Discovery**-*Learning how to look within to find your passion.*
3. **Fuel**-*What to do with your passion once you find it.*
4. **Uniqueness**-*Opinions from real life passionpreneurs and how passion beats death, stress, and can help find love.*
5. **Mental Health**-*Passion Life Cycle*
6. **Author's Testimonies**-*Stories that changed the Author's Life*

The chapters are designed to showcase passion stories, concepts, and responses to survey questions regarding passion from people all over the world. These are people I like to reference, as *"passionpreneurs"*, modern day's superstars who were willing to share their struggles to success as well as stories about how they challenged their fears and found purpose, love and passion. In addition, I have included some real life passion experiences of my own within each chapter and what each meant in my life.

If a negative situation is upon us, this book will help change and make it a positive one. The words are meant to put the readers in a different state of mind, to give you the energy to lift off, get going and begin living a life of passion and full of love. If you don't know where you're headed or just need a little push in a positive direction, you have come to the right place.

Throw logic out of the equation because logic has a way of screwing up our thoughts and leading more towards justifying our mistakes, instead of acknowledging and accepting them. Logic gives us a legitimate reason to procrastinate, be lazy, and blame society for our shortcomings. This is not saying logical thinking is a bad thing; this is saying logical thinking may prevent you from thinking realistically in a real life situation and may cause you to over think the simplicity of life.

We need to keep things simple, real and with love, not only with others but also with ourselves.

GOAL

The goal of the book is to teach humanity, explore how to get up after being knocked down and to not let obstacles keep us from going farther than we imagine. The time is now to step up and be accounted for your passion! My passion to motivate and educate is brewing in my pores and I release my positivity to the world through this book.

When I refer to passion, I am not discussing monetary rewards. I am referring to fulfillment and contentment we get from doing the things we love with the people we love, true and unconditional passion and purpose. In the current world we live in, the odds are against us, but with faith we can do all things with passion!

In addition, I recognize those individuals who searched for creative, innovative self-employment opportunities by doing something they love and helping the lives of others. You inspired the creation of my new word "passionpreneur".

The word passionpreneur comes from the 90's dream of being an entrepreneur and constant dreams of having the big house with the picket fence and the Mercedes in the drive way, but once these things where obtained, something was still missing and the birth of the passionpreneur began. I had everything but I was missing something inside of me, the picture looked great but behind the picture laid a man without a purpose. I was living a life of paying bills and going to work, every day. I wanted more and becoming a passionpreneur made sense, I wanted to have the freedom to spend six months in Barbados and six months in the United States (U.S.), but how could I change something I love to do into something financially rewarding as well?

The journey began with the creation of this book, and developing a plan to transition from my government job to my dream job without losing momentum in life. Passionpreneurs push the expectations and standards bar to the next level and look to maximize their potential and help others along the way. In addition, the word passionpreneur was created to showcase global citizens who have challenged the *status quo* and defied the odds of oppression, stereotypes, hatred, poor education, crime, depression and poverty to pursue the things they love in life.

Passionpreneurs will take a negative event and turn it into a positive No matter who is right or wrong, they are focused on providing a solution and moving forward in a positive direction, often sacrificing their own well-being for others. They don't listen to the *status quo*; they CREATE the *status quo*. Passionpreneurs sacrifice, plan and focus on the end goal of living life to the fullest with passion.

Do not walk away from dreams; they are not too big to

accomplish. We just have to come up with a strategy on how to follow our dreams and how to sustain our current way of living. The easy way out is not an option; the choice of quitting does not live in our house (mind).

This book also provides a mental point of view from Maslow, a passion survey, passion checklist and the author's personal life experiences. This information will articulate the confidence and fortitude needed to move forward in our lives and help us start over or better. Just saying "get up and get going" is not enough, but the passion we have inside us will move us in a positive direction if we learn how to awaken our passion and purpose.

This book will help us first stand up, then stand on our own, and help someone else stand up. The most rewarding after falling down is getting back up with power and then teaching someone else who has fallen how to get up.

We all are passionate about something - some know what their passion is, some guess, and some don't care. Well I care, not only for my passion but the passion of others who have continually sacrificed their time and energy to help others. I followed my passion for writing by writing this book and I have faith it will change the mindset of many. Let the passion force be with us!

PIE (PASSION IS EVERYTHING)
"I love to travel down the road that has not been created yet. Take a leap of faith and go down the path not visible."
-Oumar Hill

Think of the verb *Meraki* that means to do something with our soul, creativity, or love to put something of yourself into your work. This is passion and it makes my world go around. The world is full of passion, from the Olympics, World Cup, to the Apartheid movement in South Africa and the contestants on the American Idol singing with all the breath enclosed in their souls.

I love to see people displaying passion in the things they do for a living; it makes me feel good to see people giving their all for something they love to do and then are rewarded for their effort. I especially love the fight of the person who is not supposed to win or survive; we call these types of people "underdogs". It takes more courage, energy, faith and commitment to compete in anything, which we are foreseen to lose; it takes passion to face a giant. We live in a world full of love and hate; the fans will either love us or hate with a passion and it is nothing we can do about it. Passion will unite strangers as one to reach a common goal. Passion is powerful.

After reading several books regarding passion and noticing the real life stories within them only pertained to wealth, I decided to create a book with stories about people who are not celebrities, but are successful and popular in my heart.

When we discuss passion, the experiences of celebrities are often the only comparisons made to success and a person chasing their passion, which makes me pose the question- does this mean a person that is not rich is less passionate? No, there are people all over the world doing great things for their families and living with passion. From the single mother who has been abandoned, to the wife of a soldier who was killed in the line of duty, it takes passion and courage to start our lives over after something has been taken away from us. Passion is in everything. I have always had a passion for educating others and myself on how to get up from falling, how to do what makes us happy and not to settle.

When I was growing up, it seems money ruled the world and the television stars had the good life, until I grew up and those stars began to become broke and drugs addicts. Money was not the driving force for me as an adult. Once I acquired the nice things in life, it was not enough. I was not fulfilled and I woke up every morning empty and something was missing.

The passion and love for who I am and what I represent is what was missing. I was in search for myself and money was not the remedy; it was actually the enemy. I had to release my internal ego and turn my attitude towards what being successful really means, so I cut back on spending and living above my means to satisfy the opinions of others and society. I created my own standards and lived by them.

After receiving my graduate degree from college, I was presented the opportunity to work as an intern broker for a large investment company, long hours but I would have been making six figures straight out of college and living in New York City. But God had another plan for my life, so I decided to decline the offer and remain in my current position, open a non-profit in Prince Georges County Maryland and travel the world to learn different cultures.

I am glad I did because in a few years the U.S. was hit with one of the biggest investment scams and the company that wanted me folded. During my travel, I visited various parts of the world, Caribbean islands, Africa, Canada and Mexico, and I realized I wanted to spread the message of anything is possible to everyone community I visited. I wanted my name to represent three things: Integrity, Possibility and Passion. The more I traveled, the more I realized my life had a bigger purpose than a nice house and a car.

Sometimes we tend to live our own little world where some of us are not affected by the ills of the real world full of racism, genocide, human trafficking, sexism, hatred of homosexuals, and anti-Semitism. We only visit this "real world" if it happens in our families or immediate circle of friends, which is an ignorant blind eye to reality. Unfortunately, many people attempt to address the negativity of the world with violence and other negative responses. I decided to proactively engage this world of negativity before it reaches my family.

There are people suffering in the world and we cannot help them all but we can help some of them by instilling passion and purpose into their lives.

NO TO VIOLENCE
The Lord turn his face toward you and give you peace.
-Numbers 6:26, NIV

Violence is not the answer and neither is bitterness or retroactive violence. For example, the Michael Dunn case in Florida, which Mr. Dunn was convicted in February of 2014 of three counts of second-degree murder in the Jacksonville, FL shooting of Jordan Davis. The story is resonating with black Americans due to the previous case in Florida surrounding George Zimmermann vs. Trayvon Martin's family and subsequently being found not guilty. Whether guilty or not, we must refrain from posting retroactive bitterness on social media platforms and making jokes of the defendant.

We have to remember there are two families involved in the case and respect each family's rights. We all have the right to speak freely, but we must manage our opinions and respect the values of others during our delivery. Two wrongs do not make a right and a Facebook post will not affect the outcome, unless we utilize our responses in a peaceful and constructive way to improve the greater good of humanity. Yes, we live in a country where we value the opinion of everyone but sometimes the speakers do not use common sense.

Violence is not a black and white problem, it's a humanity problem, which needs to be changed to make the world a better place, but we cannot compound one problem with another. We must put fire (racism) out with water (peace and purpose), not fire. Last I recall, George Zimmerman is not doing too well and has been involved with the law in a few occurrences since his victory in court. The best justice in life is karma; sometimes we must pray and wait for the truth to set us free.

When a journey through a dark valley in life comes to an end, we can look to our experiences there as a guide for knowing how to help others through the same dark time.

Karma has no color; it affects people of all races. When a murder is committed both families involved (perpetrator's and victim's) will lose something and they will never be the same. Passion and compassion is needed to combat violence, depression, insecurity and maturity. Later in Chapter 3 we will discuss how to find our passion with compassion, which will go deeper into the logistics to finding our passion.

There are some things in life we will endure, which will be life changing and to get through these situation we need to be as strong as the parents of Jordan Davis and pray for forgiveness for Mr. Dunn instead of spewing hatred. At the end of the day, it will take deep passion for forgiveness in order for the world to move forward as one. We live in a world full of hurt people who hurt people.

Every mindset in the world today is created at home, whether we want to accept it or not. Don't wait until your son or daughter is facing jail time to instill love in their life; start from the day one. To me, the best ways to fight violence, racism and injustice effectively is to rally humanity and fight to change the statutes and laws in your state. This means voting and becoming more political savvy to the government rules and regulations. For example, the laws in Florida, which give the citizen the mental approval to shoot a person if they fear for their life, need to be altered and amended.

The best response to negativity is a person with a positive

attitude, a plan, and a passion to correct a wrong and make sure this does not happen to anyone else. It does not always take money to get justice; sometimes it takes passion, persistence, and the will power. Violence is a short-term fix for a mistake already committed; we need to focus on long-term solutions, which will benefit our children and grandchildren.

When I traveled to certain parts of the world, I had a chance to witness human trafficking. I was shocked and then discovered it also happens in my community in the U.S. but it is rarely discussed.

I had a sense of empathy for the women who were willing to fly to serve as maids knowing they may not return, possibly be raped, be turned into sex slaves, beaten, not paid, or maybe killed. My mind stopped for a moment when I witnessed tons of young women from the ages of 14-21 years of age waiting to catch a plane maybe to never return. This made me think of the young men and women being exploited every day in my city and asked myself, what am I doing to solve this problem? It changed my life and built a desire within me to do more in my community and possibly in the world.

I have to do more; my passion will not let me sleep unless I assist with the prevention of child trafficking and exploitation. This is a new passion for me, which will be pursued the rest of my life. I have a daughter and it would crush me to see her abused and neglected.

In order to stop events in the world like this and genocide, we need passionate people willing to fight the evils of the world, kind of like modern day superheroes – Batmen, Supermen and Wonder women with the primary purpose of creating a better humanity. Each of us has someone in our family who has been directly or indirectly affected by one of the previous; some wounds are deeper than others. In addition, some form of alcohol, crime, or incarceration has affected our families and/or friends in some way.

Think back to the moment you wished you could do something more to help that person change their life, but we have to realize the problems start at home. We must get back to being a society built on strong values and morals led by passionate parents and grandparents.

STARTS AT HOME

The world, communities and families need more passionate leaders and builders to change the direction the world is headed today. I love my family so much. Were it not for their passion and love for me to reach my success, I would never have made it to be the person I am today. I would have never become a passionpreneur if I did not have the support and push from my family and community of friends. They have always had the faith and confidence in me, that I did not always have, and it helped me get through the rainy days in my life and exceed my own expectations.

Just when the world had counted me out, my family was counting me in and their passion for my success helped me elevate my thinking. Life is difficult and unpredictable, but if we instill confidence, faith, values and morals in our children, the odds of success are in their favor. My family environment prepared me for the world by giving me self-discipline, self-confidence, self-respect, humbleness, a code of ethics for life, respect for others' beliefs, and positive relationships within the immediate community.

The love from family members and close friends builds passion and compassion. This book is geared to help us understand passion changes not only our lives, but the people around us as well. Passion is a positive addiction to living, giving and loving.

"If we keep our focus on God, we will keep our feet marching in the right direction when those around us go sideways."-Oumar Hill

    Happiness is what we all should be working towards, not social status or money; if we are passionate about our work those things will come with commitment and perseverance. Chip Conley's book, Simple Truths for Creating Happiness + Success: Emotional Equations includes equations on emotions, the likes of emotions = life or Joy =Love-Fear, which is true because most things we love we also fear, but the less fear we have the more love and ultimately the more joy we will have in our life. We must eliminate all the fear in our life to live a joyful life - be fearless!

    However, my favorite equations by Mr. Conley is "Happiness = wanting what you have/Having what you want and Happiness= Practicing Gratitude/Pursuing Gratification, Faith= Belief/Intellect." I place these equations on my vision board to help remind myself of the simple things in life - my wants versus my needs and how important my faith is to my success. These equations helped me understand my passion and life in general

    I implore all of my clients who have an ounce of doubt to follow their dreams and live with purpose. When I think of living with passion I think of the Dafna Michealson's story. This single mom quit her regular day job and took her journey to 50 states across the U.S. to uncover the stories of amazing people who are making a difference in their community but are simultaneously under the radar of stardom. She captured over 375+ videos, helping people all over the world, co-founded The Journey Institute and wrote a book about her journey.

    She could have quit but something with her inner core pushed her to do and want more. She could have not cared about her fellow citizens in Denver who were experiencing hardship but she did, she had feelings for her community and took the imitative to do something about. She did not just focus on her personal wellbeing but the wellbeing of others. She then figured out a way to share the stories of so many Americans who are doing great things in their respective communities around the world.

This not only helped the person telling the story but also subliminally helped her and others who viewed the videos.

"Sometimes your medicine bottle has on it, shake well before using. That is what God has to do with some of his people. He has to shake them well before they are ever usable"
-Vance, Havner

Blessings all around, when we lead with passion. Ms. Michealson extended a helping hand, sacrificed her own time and energy and in return has been blessed with her passion and purpose in life. To me she is the prime example of a passion pioneer, who faced her fear headfirst and we need to follow her footsteps in life.

INTERVIEW: DOMESTIC VIOLENCE SURVIVOR

One of the most touching and heart felt stories I have ever witnessed was the one of a young lady working with me as a contractor. She was very cute, stylish and was a sight to see, married with kids and happy, it seemed. Inside she was screaming for help and assistance to get out of a marriage that was mentally, physically and spiritually abusive. I had a chance to sit and talk with this young lady about how she faced domestic violence and won, it was an awesome conversation.

We never know how our simple hellos and listening skills can help someone get through turmoil; human beings have to stop turning their backs on their neighbors and give their undivided attention to them without the expectation of reward. If we give a little time and energy we never know how much we are helping the individual venting the problem and developing a plan.

This is not saying entertain negativity, but listen to a person describe their problem and then help them get through it. Now if they are continuously complaining and not looking for a way out, they might not be ready for assistance. The best person to help a person in a stressful situation is himself or herself.

There will come a time where we need to focus on investing more time in the community instead of figuring ways to manipulate the system and community for our selfish intentions. Her story moved me, helped me share it with women going through the same situation. Domestic violence is sadly a common problem in my community Prince Georges County, Maryland.

Listen to how she managed to utilize her focus, determination and faith to get out of the situation, do better and keep her kids strong during the process. Now she is happily married, has become her own *passionpreneur* opening her own business and living her dream.

1. **What are the signs of domestic violence?**
   There will be occasions where we can identify the traits of an abusive individual right away; i.e., anger issues or an explosive temper, lack of communication skills, upbringing (abusive parent(s)), excessive habits (drinking, drugs, etc.). Most times the signs are hidden and women tend to overlook them, being blinded by infatuation, and misinterpretations of love, lust, financial dependence or the involvement of children.

2. **How can a woman prevent being a victim of domestic violence?**
   Prevention lies within "getting to know" and "taking off the blinders". Women must learn how to promote, demand, enforce and defend having effective communication skills.

Don't be afraid to ask the important questions of who, what, where this guy comes from before getting too involved.

Secondly, get some standards and be firm about them; don't allow his persuasive character or physical looks to break your standards (men only do what women allow them to). It's more than ok to have a "realistic" checklist when it comes to bringing a partner into your life. Always know that you deserve and can achieve better and if he does not measure up, let him go. The guy for you is definitely out there.

3. **What do I tell my daughter to do if she experiences domestic violence?**

   If she does, God forbid, becomes a victim of domestic violence, let her know that it is not the result of something she did or that she can fix within him. Tell someone, at her job, a friend, family member, doctor, someone. Do not have the expectation that the person she has chosen to inform about her situation can and will save her from the volatile relationship.

   However, they may be able to give or lead her to great advice and resources to "help" her help herself; it is then up to her to take that advice and utilize it. Be smart about the exit plan that she chooses, meaning; keep her plan to herself (don't tell the kids, if they're involved). Stick to the plan and NEVER revert back. The most important tools that will aid her in recognizing, preventing and surviving domestic violence, are mental and spiritual strength.

4. **Why not tell the kids?**

   Not telling the kids was something that I chose to do in *my* situation. There were several factors:

a. They were young in age and their father had the ability to manipulate information out of them, in turn he would then have the opportunity to sabotage my exit strategy. This is where the controlling trait kicks in. Never lie to your kids; we just do not have to discuss everything with them. Keep them in a child's place.
b. I wanted to minimize as much mental damage on them as possible, keep their childhood intact. It would decrease the time spent in therapy (my oldest two have gone to therapy in regards to the divorce and it helped immensely!). The abuser and abused failed to understand the children are affected as well in a domestic dispute (divorce, etc.). The chains have to be broken and as a parent, it begins with me giving them the opportunity to grow into healthy adults.
c. Even though my relationship has ended with their father, I never wanted to ingrain my children with negative feelings or thoughts of their dad. If they were to ever dislike him, it would be on their individual terms. Having the child maintain a healthy relationship is vital, if you still want the other parent to remain active in the child's life. This may not apply to every domestic violence situation, some are more severe and the abusive parent may need to be permanently removed.

5. **I love the fact you touched on the Mental Health topic. Elaborate on how mental and spiritual faith helped you get through this ordeal.**

    a. During this period of turmoil, you are broken mentally and spiritually. Your entire being is incarcerated and the warden is your abuser. It's very easy to place blame on one's self, absorbing all responsibility and not having the will or strength to fight back (intelligently).

As young girls growing up, we are taught to be submissive, honor and obey our husbands or the man in your life. No one tells the same young girls that when said man abuses this trait within you and does not deserve, it's ok to no longer submit and support. Some faiths even speak against divorce in this situation. So, as the woman, we begin to question our faith, beliefs and thoughts. Some will abandon them all together.

b. Mental and Spiritual Strength is the *only* tool/weapon you have that can fight back and win. Strengthen your spirituality to make your mind stronger. Your thoughts (subconscious and conscious) have a direct and indirect impact on your life situation, Law of Attraction. You have to believe that what's occurring is wrong, 100%!

Only you have the power to change it. Take responsibility for what you've done to put yourself in this predicament. Yes, each party involved is a contributor to the situation, just in different ways. I was once told that; 90-95% of happenings in our life are due to a direct/indirect decision made on our part. Understand that, own it and live by it. This will also help in future relationships

c. Once you've become ironclad strong mentally and spiritually; you have taken back the power. He can't harm you anymore. You are now thinking with a clear mind, a positive mind. You are open to and ready for change. Your agility has been restored; and you are able to make the right decisions and moves to bring you out of the situation.

d. Having these strengths helped preserve the great woman that I am, so I can share myself with the right man. The deserving man. Many women that survive domestic violence also become lifetime victims, because they are damaged. Every abusive man I have talked to over the years has mentioned the following statement,

"If I can't have you, no one else can", whether he meant it as to end her physical life on this earth or metaphorically. He still wins, either way.

6. **When he's home what do you do, what's next?**
    a. Get out of the house, if possible
    b. Call the cops, tell the kids to dial 911, or a neighbor
    c. Have him removed from the house with a restraining order and enforce it.
    d. There are many programs that offer shelter to women and women with kids. They have hotlines; emergency rooms will assist any woman in need with this information. The program will pay for transportation to pick you up and your destined location will not be made public.

7. **What are the key elements to getting back to loving yourself and knowing you are worthy of Queen-ship?**

    a. I've never stopped loving myself; I just didn't put my love for self-first. Again, this will vary from woman to woman. I've asked several ladies this question and some with deeper issues like; childhood abuse (physically, mentally, sexually); alcohol abuse; drug abuse; etc., were more likely to respond stating "they didn't love themselves, and

didn't know how to without the help of a professional".
b. The mental and spiritual strength is the key element. Pair this with counseling, and she'll be unstoppable.
c. Queen was always there, the foundation anyway. It's tough to experience what was intended and started out to be a beautiful life, get turned upside down and blown to pieces; and not appear to be disheveled. There were a handful of males who helped me (directly and indirectly), including YOU, to get me where I am today. Thank you for giving me the opportunity to share my experience and gifting it to prevent domestic violence with others.
.

Message from this chapter: *It's never too late to follow your dreams, you just have to determine what the most important thing in your life is and then love it for the rest of your life. Love with a passion.*

-SECTION I: DISCOVERY-

Let's get all into you, who are you?

CHAPTER 1: DIG DEEPER

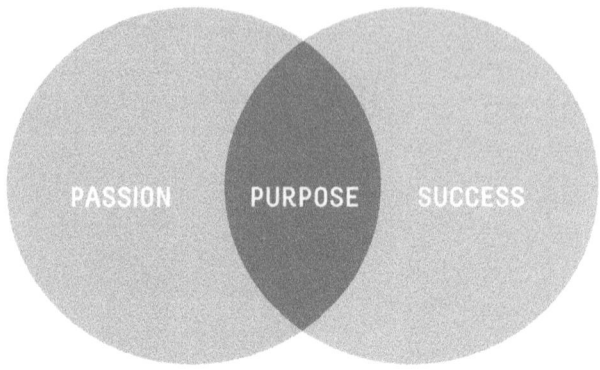

Trust in the Lord with all your heart, and lean not on your own understanding; in all your ways acknowledge him, and he shall direct your paths

DIVE INTO YOU

Why is the world focused on happiness? Is it because of the bad economy, war and poverty throughout the world? Maybe because of the increase in violence in public places, which are presumed to be safe, possibly? Moreover, maybe it's the result of a generation of parents chasing money only to realize the lack of value money has versus happiness, which is priceless.

I remember attending Howard University and I switched majors from business to occupational therapy then to physical therapy. Heck in college, the mindset of most students I hung around was, let's find a major which will make us some money, we don't have to take too many standardized test and we don't have to be in college for 8 years especially, if we were already in a Medical or Law related program. The mission was to find a major to graduate with, which could get us a job making six figures in the

90's.

Therapy was okay because it involved helping someone regain his or her way of living in some kind of way, but it did not fulfill me, it still felt like a job. I did not think about what I would want to do until retirement. In my early 20's I was more concerned with establishing myself amongst my peers and obtaining the finer things in life, rarely did I invest or think about creating a business for myself and creating generational wealth.

Only after trials and tribulation, traveling abroad, having a daughter, meeting new people, learning new careers, and revisiting what makes me happy from childhood could I make a definite decision to say, "I want to do this particular task for the rest of my life". We all have the choice to take the easy road or the long road to success, I decided to create my own road and though it has been tough, others will be able to follow my road once I am finished building. The goal in my life is to serve as an example of possibility and never quitting on myself. I am no different from any male born in America or Africa, I just have more opportunities.

DREAMS ARE REAL

What have we always thought about doing? Who have we always dreamed of becoming? What places in the world have we dreamed of living? What would we sacrifice for happiness? Want to live on a farm, beach or city? We should be able to answer these questions in a positive light once we complete reading this book.

Too often in life we settle for instant gratification, instead of waiting and learning from our gut - our true emotions and feelings about the things in life we want to do. It is similar to a single person with the "timeline disease", meaning by a certain date I want to be married, have a child, get a house and travel the world. But then life throws the individual a "curve ball" and the person has a choice to make - do I (1) settle for the next thing coming so I can satisfy my personal ego or (2) do I understand my timeline has been extended. I would suggest the latter; settling for something we really do not want will eventually lead to problems in the person, business and/or relationships.

When we settle for things, we lose valuable pieces of our passion and purpose. We cannot settle to satisfy the needs of others; we must communicate our needs and work together to make sure we satisfy each other's needs. To find and obtain our passion we need complete focus and commitment to sustain our energy and faith in the process. Dreams are possible, but their success begins with you.

WHEN I GROW UP?

One problem within the inner city or suburbs next door to the inner city is the world within the world. There is the real world and there is the world we live in, for many this may be hard to comprehend but I will try to articulate.

My mother and father created a great world for me full of promise, favor and wisdom but the other world I lived in was the world with my street friends and we did not think we were going to make it to the age of 25 years old. I was lucky because I had a strong family base but growing up in Prince Georges County and Washington DC we often assimilated with the problems our friends had because we were a team and a collective group. Some of my friends had the opportunity to associate with the rich kids or intellectual kids at a young age to see the different opportunities in the world versus a kid from the hood (low-income area) whose options were far and few between.

So the question regarding what we wanted to be when we grow up was kind of farfetched because we did not think we would make it to be grown. The majority of the successful people around us were either on the basketball or football field and there were others who were successful in their profession but they were not celebrated as much as the athletes and movie stars. For a young male, the world was full of opportunities but we just could not see it because some of us where submerged in the laws of the street forming a mind frame of not thinking about investing, building wealth and accumulating wealth over numerous investments because we were merely trying to survive and make a living now.

Luckily I had a father who was there every step of my journey and a mother who refused to let me fail, even when I wanted to fail myself. I just want to disclose the world within a world concept to help people trying to teach kids about their future, opportunities and creating a career. When we are trying to teach our kids, we have to build a platform, which speaks to their current environment so that they will receive our teaching and visually see the way to success. I always tell kids when I travel, "You can be whatever you want, but you have to decide when you want it and how bad you want it", then I always modify my next sentence to relate to the circumstances that particular individual is going through.

I would change the question from what do you want to be when you grow up to what happens when you live past 25? 35? 45? What do you want to do when you are 60? If I asked most juvenile delinquents what the LSAT or MCAT was they would think it is a new form of drug similar to LSD, not to say they aren't intelligent, but just consumed in their environment.

If we want to change the thought process in the minority community, we need to curtail our teaching to reach our kids and not only teach them. Kids just need a plan and the ability to see that plan to fruition. The kids in the inner city want a better life, and just need more people to help them understand them better amidst the trials and tribulations they are currently living in to pursue their passion. Passion to them is surviving today and now,

now in 20 years.

Again, I was blessed to have a strong foundation of family members raised in the southern parts of the U.S., who had faced oppression and supported me regardless of my faults. They put me in a mentally positive situation and exposed me to the other opportunities in the world.

One of my favorite childhood memories is my elementary (grade) schoolteacher, Mrs. Williams, asking me "what do you want to be when you grow up". I can remember the puzzled and happy faces of some of my classmates. When I was a kid we just wanted to go outside and have play time. Some were prepared by their parents, siblings and mentors to know what to say. While, others did not have the family support and role models to prepare them for this question and had the "deer in the headlights" look.

Luckily, I was raised in a family that preached greatness and possibility; anything less than great was unacceptable. I had choices and I could back up each career with substantial information to make you believe I was headed in that direction. At this age, I did not know I would have the opportunity to create six books in one year, travel to Africa multiple times and speak various languages.

Today, I wanted to be the same person I told my friends twenty-five years ago, "I just want to be the best me." I was taught I could do whatever I wanted to do. If wanted to do acting, I did it. If I wanted to be basketball coach, I did it. Now I did not just go and do it without a plan. I created a plan to put me in a successful position and make a contribution to the people I encountered.

Although, I was primed to answer the question of what I wanted to be when I grew up, I was not trained to follow my passion. I was trained to go to school, get good grades, try to stay out of trouble, and get a good job. I was exposed to the art of becoming an entrepreneur in college, which is why I birthed the concept of the passionpreneur.

Back to the chapter topic, some kids say they want to be sport stars, but after a series of discussions with my grandparents I realized the life span of a sports super hero was short and I wanted to live forever. Nonetheless, this is not a typical response for a kid to have to this kind of question because kids, by nature, are very competitive, and at a young age all we really know is how to be a kid; they are continuously on a path to try to find their identity. I call it the lions determining who is the highest on the kindergarten food chain to get peanut butter and jelly sandwiches or who is the coolest in the class.

When I was asked the question, I was ready to impress, I was going to say a lawyer or doctor, take my LSAT or MCAT and go to a top rated college. I was sure to raise a few eyebrows, but deep down in my heart my passion was to serve people. But how could I make a living giving myself to people? (It took me 30 years to figure this out.) I told the class my intent. Some were smiling, while others smirked although they were impressed. Thought I was the most impressive, I felt empty inside because I did not tell the truth about my passion to be a servant and leader of the people.

But then the most memorable kid stepped up unscripted and said, "I want to be a tennis instructor". All the kids laughed at him, but he was not amused. This kid went to college on a tennis scholarship and played professional tennis for a few years. I guess he got the last laugh. My classmate was determined to show the people who doubted him who he really was. I learned that day, it didn't matter how I was perceived by my peers it was more important that I stand up for what I believed in.

As kids, we are not subjected to all the intricacies the world has to offer and only after subjecting ourselves to the positive and negative events, people and places in the world, will we definitely come up with something we truly find happiness in doing. This does not mean a person will graduate from high school or college and not be able to find a good job, make a lot of money and become a superstar. This simply means if we are searching for what really makes us happy; we must look past money, fame, and social acceptance and look into our heart to see what drives us.

Achieving happiness and fulfillment in our life by pursuing what makes us smile and feel fulfilled is a blessing in itself. We all are worthy of accomplishing great things, but very few of us actually pursue these things due to fear and insecurity. A setback is actually a setup; rejections are actually opportunities to be accepted somewhere else. Quitting is not an option; we will have another chance to win in the game of life, we just need to prepare and be ready.

Following our passion and dreams is a very bold and courageous act, which will require discipline, commitment, and energy to complete. I am very passionate about helping people find their happiness and the creation of this book is phase one; www.passionpreneur.com is phase two. The new concept will change lives and perspectives on passion.

PASSION PERSPECTIVE

Passion is a strong feeling of enthusiasm or excitement for something or about doing something: a strong feeling (such as anger) that causes you to act in a dangerous way: a strong sexual or romantic feeling for someone.

Passion is a variety of emotions. Passion can be the feeling we get when we are going through a rough period of our life. It can be the feeling you get to finish a task that keeps you from eating and sleeping, like a musician traveling the country away from family and friends to pursue their dreams and create generational wealth for their families.

It could also be a father fighting for a country to change its concept and ideologies of freedom by subjecting his life to twenty-seven years in a South African prison, thereby changing not only the minds of the government, but also the world, thanks to the late Nelson Mandela. It could be a young kid born in Atlanta, GA, who had a dream amongst the violence in the world against his color and still had the strength inside to follow his dream and bring it to fruition.

Passion will take us places where we never could have imagined going. I can only think of how Jay-Z feels now when he sits and contemplates his journey from Brooklyn to the top of the world. When he was younger running the streets of Brooklyn something clicked in him to sacrifice, dig deep, and not settle for girls, money, cars and VIP status at the club as some rappers have chosen. Instead, Jay-Z had a vision and wanted more and his passion led him to greatness, a legacy to go down in the record books.

Who could have imagined with the predecessors of Biggie Smalls and Tupac Shakur? I think Jay-Z's passion to tell his life story through music and mentally provide therapy to his listeners all across the world is his purpose. I think his purpose is to lead whether it is the world, his family and friends to a better place of consciousness, happiness and fulfillment through not only music, but also working hard and overachieving, not settling for the average.

Another example of passion superstar who has changed the world is the slender Caribbean kid born in Jamaica only to become a world and motivational icon for kids forty years after his death. **Nesta Robert Marley** also known, as *Bob Marley* has been one of the most internationally loved music stars in the world. His music relates to all people from various races. Coming from Saint Ann Parish in Jamaica, who would have thought this young man would bring together people through music and reduce racial tension between different races helping to unify the world through his voice? His passion to stand up for something bigger than himself, believe in himself, and to see outside of our box, is epic and has yet to be duplicated. Passion will help a person forget about their "troubles in the world".

If we lead with passion, our potential is limitless only if we remain focused and disciplined. If we don't we will be mentally boxed in by the limitations project on us by others and ourselves.

It's ironic that most successful people don't only think about themselves they think about the others around them. Trying to leave our comfortable job to move to a third world country may seem crazy to some, but when we come back smiling, happy and energetic because we have freedom, peace and serenity, maybe people will change their mind. Some people are afraid of taking the first step to change their circumstances. Avoid being this type of person. When following passion, time will be of our least concern; we will get to work early and leave late.

Please understand there is an inherent danger when you are following your passion. You will always face adversity, but you have to remember that passion has an energy all of its own and it is infectious. For example, most top college basketball teams in the U.S. have at least one person on the team who just breathes passion. In fact, all of the top teams in any sport have at least one or two players on the team that practice, play and execute with passion. This passion is the greatness that makes their teammates work harder and overachieve; consequently, everyone around them becomes a better player - like Michael Jordan and the Chicago bulls of the 80's. A team full of passion is a team ready for a championship, whether in basketball or business. Teams that work together passionately are prone to be successful.

PASSION ZONE

When I followed my passion of writing and informing people of the truth about passion, I often forgot to eat, cut off a few friends, reduced leisure activities, and focused on the completion of this book. I was officially in my passion zone.

The passion zone is similar to a sports commentator referencing a basketball player who has made a numerous amounts of shots or great plays, "He is on fire!" The passion zone is where we begin to gain confidence in our ability, the vision is becoming clear, and we gain discipline from our old ways.

My passion zone is what kept me home for the holidays to finish writing this book instead of going to Barbados or South Africa. I say most individuals go in and out of their passion zone. As kids we are passionate about learning how to read, walk, talk, write and socialize to please our parents, and then it continues in high school when we are passionate about learning how to become an adult and how to develop our skills. As we get closer to graduating from high school and college we begin to think about our internal passion deeply.

When you are in your zone, nothing will stop you or deter you from your passion. The biggest hurdles in my life were the following: trying to do everything at one time, trying be everything to everybody and learning how to say no. Often times when we get the confidence and stamina to accomplish success we think we can do it all. In the next chapter we will discuss having multiple passions in detail and provide a solution to help you manage your passions better.

MUTILPLE PASSION-ITIS

Do you suffer from this disease? If so I have an aged old remedy that can cure you today. I wanted to be a lawyer, actor, fisherman, CEO, then a shark hunter and many more things. It's okay we can have multiple emotions about different things to do; we are human.

The key to passion is similar to the search for love. We must search for love not lust; do not confuse the things we lust for with the things we love. The emotions have similarity but one is temporary and will eventually dissolve versus the other, which is a lifelong bond never to be broken. Passion is engraved in our gut, while lust is engraved in other areas of our body, depending on the intentions of our internal needs.

Is it possible to have multiple passions at the same time? Yes, I have a passion for my career, family, extended family, leisure activity, and for the health of humanity. Now at some point we may encounter a passion conflict. If this happens, we need to prioritize which passion is first and make ethically correct decisions.

Sub-passions are endeavors we undertake to roll up into our passion goal or purpose in life. For example, I am passionate about helping people all over the world improve their life and learn how to get up after falling in life. My sub-passions included the development of a nonprofit, public speaking, creation of this book, mentoring kids in Washington, DC, going to Africa to help with a documentary, handing out turkeys during Thanksgiving, coaching a youth basketball team, serving as a role model on social websites, and being a great father. All of these roles helped me mature into the person I am today, pure motivation.

Passion is a hard thing to do sometimes; but when it's real, we will sacrifice everything. Passion is the feeling we have inside which makes us feel good, loved, and self-worthy. It helps us go to sleep, wake up, and get our days started.

I remember when I decided to pursue a career in acting - oh yes I wanted to be a star! I had never been to an acting school, coach or participated in drama class in high school; it was all pure raw acting from growing up as the neighborhood clown. I went into an audition and said a few words. The director said, "Okay, great! See you on Monday. Wear this and that." I was shocked at the acceptance but later realized that being awarded a role, as an extra on an HBO show was not so great and hard work! But, it was exciting and something new, which fueled my curiosity and passion. I loved doing something new and fresh; it kept me intrigued and wanting to learn more.

Then the phone rang, it was for a bigger role, but it was a role I was not prepared to commit due to my commitment to my nonprofit and the kids I served. The money was awesome and it was a great opportunity, but I decided it was not the priority in my life at the moment. Acting was not my passion and it was something within me, which said, "This is not for me, regardless of the financial reward". I still act every once in a while but more for mental health and to release my inner Steven Seagal.

POSITIVE AND NEGATIVE PASSION

Life is all about balance; so if we have positive, then there must be negativity lurking around somewhere waiting to be discovered. Think about it, the mind of a serial killer has something inside him pushing him to a level of mental instability and he believes in his thoughts so much that he acts upon them. Though it is devilish in nature, it is a form of passion. Barbaric in purpose, but it is an internal emotion that drives a person to an act.

If we fully understand the emotions that drive a person to kill another, we could possibly prevent the act from happening. This is the reason FBI agents utilize the historical data on a potential suspect to understand the complete mental profile of the individual.

Positive examples of passion are people who use their God given talents to help others. For example, Bill Gates the creator of Microsoft has a passion bigger than computer codes and fancy gadgets. He is a well-known philanthropist, who is accompanied with his wife and contributes to various worldwide campaigns to fight hunger, HIV, educational awareness, genocide, and countless other humanitarian efforts.

Are we prepared to help others the right way? To fully understand our passion, we have to be real with ourselves. We can only grow if we understand ourselves for not only our positive but our negative attributes as well. Once we know how to ignite the fire, whether good or bad, we have more control over the entire landscape of our passion.

We can use our negative passion to be reinforcements or drivers for the positive outputs. For example, when I was a kid, I was very outgoing to say the least and would get into trouble at least once a day. My parents did not hesitate to reinforce their positive passion about me growing into a productive citizen by enforcing negative passion on my buttocks by way of a leather belt and their passion was well received.

CHANGE A NEGATIVE TO A POSITIVE

We all know someone in our family or a friend in jail or trouble with the law. Crime is very serious. In order to change the cycle of creating criminals, we must change their perspective and turn their negative passion into positive passion. We must find a way to use the skills we have and use these skills in a constructive way. More money equals more problems, but more people doing what they love and living with happiness will create a culture of love. Compassion is a part of the passion process and will help bring stability to our lives.

To change the system, we must create a system full of love and compassion. This program must start from the day of incarceration, and everyone involved has a role to play. The family will have to provide a positive stimulus. Likewise, the correctional facility and the inmate must all work towards a common goal to change their life, and become passionate about something positive. I have a childhood friend who was incarcerated, but has used his incarceration to serve as a positive talking point to prevent young men from making the same mistakes he did since his release. For him, the idea of being placed in a box is not life, and its mind breaking. Freedom was the most important thing he enjoyed. The freedom to speak, love, and travel, had more value than money; so prior to his release he dedicated his life to Christ and dedicated himself to furthering his education. Sometime we have to go through hell to get to heaven; never give up on your community, because some of our most productive leaders today were bad teenagers.

We must find things in our life that propel us towards our passion, things in our life where we plant seeds. Like fruit we need **"passion seeds"** to nourish, monitor and learn from them, so the seeds can turn into fruit. It is the "passion fruit" that gives us the fuel to begin the passion equation.

Once the passion equation is started, it becomes hard to resist the urge to learn, explore and discover more about it. Once I breached the passion zone, my pursuit of it was then initiated. This rush for happiness and fulfillment is when we mentally think we are in love, or when a soccer player is about to score a goal to win the game with seconds left on the clock - pure adrenaline, desire, commitment, focus, and self-discipline. This can be applied to your career, relationship, religion and etc. Passion is in everything we do.

(-)Negative actions+ positive passion (belt) + passion angels + positive community leadership + self-education= Positive Outcomes

PURPOSE

Purpose is the reason for which something is done or created or for which something exists. Purpose is life and passion is the fuel that feeds life. To be successful we need both and we need to understand them. Purpose is why I reach out to my friends in Namibia and wish them well or why millions of people send money to the Philippine to help aid the families after the traumatic storm that hit the area in 2013. Purpose is what defines who we are, what we stand for, and what our legacy will represent. It is my purpose that aligns me with heaven or hell. My passion will eventually lead me to my purpose; so if my passion is positive, I will have a positive purpose and vice versa.

Passion+ faith + Providence= Purpose

The equation above illustrates how I was able to find my true purpose in life. I had to first find my true passion, and once I found my passion I had to have faith in the process and trust the things happening in my life have already been predetermined (Providence). Through this process I found my true meaning for living, hence the birth of my purpose. Purpose is often bigger than anything we could ever imagine, and each person in the world has a role to play. The world is an orchestra and we are all playing different tunes, but working for the same composer. Life is short and we need to maximize our potential, make it a career, and show others how to do it.

GET UP

One day, I was relaxing on the beach in Barbados, listening to the ocean wind blow, and thinking about passion and purpose. Something about being next to the ocean makes me think about all the bad times in my life and how blessed I am to get a tan. It made me feel like I never gave up on my dreams and being by the ocean is my reward.

We have all encountered life's trials & tribulations, but some of us have found a way to "Just get up." My mother would say this when I played football. I could hear her scream; "Just get your butt up," not knowing this one act would save my life in my later years of life.

We live in a world full of failure, hate, and disappointment, but yet we can find purpose and passion to help us through the rough times. I remember when I was a project manager for a contractor and they came in the office and let me go (fired me) because of my salary, I made too much money. I was floored but I kept my composure and kindly departed the premises. I told myself, this was a blessing in disguise and I was supposed to learn from this. I did, the contractor called me back within a week to offer me the position back with more pay, but I was also offered a job in the government from two separate agencies within the same week. Sometimes we just have to have faith until God determines it's time for us to go to the next level.

I agree with **Dr. Maurice Lee,** one my distinguished *passionpreneurs* who participated in the passion survey (*Hint: in later chapter*), He stated, "a successful person is the individual who has fallen down 10 times but got up 11", slowly but surely managing to get wiser and stronger each time they fell. Now some fall on purpose and others fall by mistake. A person who falls by mistake will not make the same mistake twice, while the others seem to continuously fall. I call this learning and leading yourself from failure.

Passion cannot be pursued lying down; we have to get up, go get success, it will not come to us. Consider the underdog who had very little chance of winning but for some reason, won somehow because he did not quit. I consider my life a success story, because I have been knocked down several times and even rejected, but I never gave up and found another way to reach my goals. Thinking back to high school again, I was a B+ grade foreign language student, but now I am familiar with speaking various languages. Thankful I was granted the opportunity to travel abroad and interact with the locals, who accepted me in their family and taught me their languages and culture.

How we start out in life is very important but not as half important as how we finish. If we make a mistake, it is okay; find a way, develop a plan and move forward with our purpose. Our mistakes are merely a testimony to share with our family, friends and community to help them overcome the same obstacles. I have a story about my mom facing cancer (*Hint: last chapter in this book*) and how that played a role in my purpose in life. We never know what people are going through and sometimes we will never know until we share sensitive information about ourselves. People will release information more freely when they have information about us, most times.

Spike Lee said it best, "I did not find film, film found me". I agree with Spike Lee; I did not grow up thinking I would write a book or become a motivational speaker, it found me and I liked it. We never know how our life will turn out, but we know we have to work hard at being something worthy of greatness. According to *Dr. Susan Biali,'s article* titled "The Five Steps to Finding Your Passion", the following five steps will help you discover passion:

1. Inventory your talents
2. Pay attention to what makes you annoyed or jealous.
3. Think of what you loved to do as a child.
4. Notice when you lose track of time, or what you hate to stop doing
5. See your passion hunt as a fun, joyful adventure.

For each individual reader the steps may vary and this example is only a base for you to use or develop your own steps towards finding your passion. In Chapter three, we will discuss specific steps on how to find our passion, but remember our success is dependent on our determination, discipline and faith.

Message from this chapter: *Don't be afraid to fall in love with who you are, where you are and who you are going to become. Things will happen for the better, just trust the process. Never give up on your dreams or yourself.*

CHAPTER 2: FIND IT WITH-IN

"When you wake up feel your chest, heartbeat and breath. Ok good, you're alive, God is not done with you yet. Find your passion!"
Oumar Hill

This chapter will capture the key elements of how to find passion in the things we do and love. We go through life searching for something to warm our hearts and sometimes we get distracted. It is understandable things will come up in our lives that are out of our control. We will focus our attention on what our passion actually is, pursuing it and then what to do with our passion.

Then we will discuss the importance of failure not being an option when searching for passion. "The good pushes us towards our passion; however the bad stops us dead in our tracks" (Beck, Martha). Every day needs to be enjoyed, adored, and maximized because life is too short. To find our passion means to find happiness in the things we do every day, which also keeps us productive citizens. Some of us are content with where we are in life and that is okay, but there are others whom are still searching for some type of personal fulfillment to satisfy their personal interest.

We will have success in our lives, once we focus on living a positive and honest life. We will discuss the word passionpreneur and its meaning further in Chapters 6 and 7 but here is a brief definition to help understand the concept.

Passionpreneurs are people who seek out happiness instead of wealth, still in search of freedom and opportunity but for a greater good; business ventures that not only satisfy a financial need but also help them reach the level of self-actualization. These individuals are led by fulfillment and not by financial gain, even though financial wellness will overflow with pursuing passion.

FIND IT

Passion is always one dream, step, or change away. We are humans forever growing and learning new things each day. Finding our passion is a journey, but well worth it, it awakened my spirit to pursue teaching, motivational speaking, and humanitarian work. Think if we love what we are doing we tend to behave positively towards others.

How can a person find their passion and wants out of life? To find our passion, we first have to find ourselves and work towards finding our purpose in life. Once we find what we love, we can create a realistic plan on how to achieve our passion; but it is not that easy. I am in the business of building passionpreneurs one mind at a time. Passion discovered is often hard to lose, but passion never found is often hard to discover.

We will need to dig deep into our talents from childhood and our current selves. Some questions I always ask myself when looking deep into my passion: What makes me smile? What do I want out of life? What do I want my legacy to be? Who am I? Then when I find something I love to do, I must create a plan of action and follow through with my passion. How can I get paid for doing something I love? How bad do I want it? What is my timeline for the transition?

Most of us cannot just quit our jobs abruptly to pursue our passion, so we need to methodically plan our next steps to make sure our dreams are pursued. Unfortunately, we put off our own happiness to help others achieve their happiness. How can a person without something direct another individual to something they never had? This is why it is critical to find happiness and passion for ourselves, so we can help someone else. It only takes one step to get our passion moving in the right direction towards purpose.

I would like to have the opportunity to work from home six months and the from the beach the remaining six months out of the year and enjoy the simple pleasures of life, without having to check in at a nine to five job. This is a critical piece to fulfilling our dreams of living a life of purpose and making a decision of what we really want to do in life.

If we lead with passion, no matter the trials and tribulations, our underlying passion will lead us to our destiny and reveal the happiness within us to live a productive life. We can be micromanagers of our destiny; but most of our final outcomes are out of our control. Here is where our faith has to be strong, because we have to trust the process and things will work out for the best.

I have listed below steps helped me find my passion for creating this book and becoming a motivational speaker.

A. UNDERSTAND WE ARE ENOUGH

1. **We are worthy.** We have to understand we are more than enough and that with discipline and persistence, we are more than capable of doing anything we desire. We have to mentally get to a place of undeniable conviction and boldness to go places and acquire things we never could have dreamed of. It will take hard work but the journey is worth it because we are worth it. We have been placed on the earth and should give back to it, not continuously take from it.

   Once we have this understanding of self-worthiness we can begin to question our intentions to follow our passion. What is driving us to look for more out of life? If money lost value what profession would we do for free? This is where we need to start looking for our hints that lead us to our passion. The love of money is the root of all evil and we are looking for purpose, happiness, and joy. I say this to state, "If we lead with passion and purpose, the

money will eventually come as a result of our hard work and passionate efforts." I forced myself to think about the following questions:
   a. If money did not have value what would I do for a living?
   b. What are my top priorities in life?
   c. If I had 12 months to live what would I do?
   d. What did I love to do as a kid?
   e. What makes me smile out of control?

After answering these questions it gave me a sense of what I wanted to do and a baseline to start planning my next steps.

2. **Conduct research.** So many of us get a vision but FAIL to follow through with the idea because we do not want to do the grunt work. I know some brilliant lazy people who have the best ideas but lack the reactiveness and energy to go after their dreams. Some are scared of success, failure and change, while others would rather live off of others dreams, instead of their own, too much for failure.

    The best thing I did to follow my passion is learn the ends and outs in my field and knowing the techniques my predecessors utilized to become successful. The simple art of learning, networking and collaborating with others to learn more about something we are passion about is a win-win situation.

    I became a sponge to all those who were willing to give me their pros and cons of the motivational speaking business. Research not only helps us become well versed in our craft but also shares a holistic view of our field just in case we have second thoughts and need to reconsider what really is our true passion.

3. **Set up goals and objectives.** We need to set goals for finding our passion or pursuing it. This is very important to holding ourselves accountable to making our passion and reality. As we set our goals and objectives and begin to map out our plan to find our passion, we are simultaneously building our self-esteem and confidence. Once we see it, record it and review it to make sure our plan is feasible, instant smiles and confidence will run through our pores.

    Goals are not only important to big corporations but too personal endeavors as well. We need to have complete traceability into our passion so if necessary we can go back and revise certain steps. Once we have clear milestones and deliverables for our journey we are ready to start the journey to finding our passion.

4. **Something sparked your interest.** Something has provoked us to look deeper inside of ourselves and locate what really makes us tick. This can be a tedious process because we are so submerged in our daily activities, it can be difficult to look back and determine what made us happy, but if we remember our passion in childhood then we have a one-step advantage on everyone else.

    First, I would look at my current life and whether it was something within my current career, which sparked my interest for living a complete life. Then I would look at the things I do in my leisure activity and determine if those activities are bringing me more joy than my regular job. My third review would be to go back into my childhood by visiting old neighborhoods, friends, high school and special places in my youth and see if those experiences spark a memory or a passionate thought.

    Passion does not have to be in all of our lives but somewhere along our journey we have been subjected to a passionate people more times than none. When we review these areas, we should pray about our journey and this may also lead us into our passion. Once we find something that sparked our passion, we should record the idea so we don't lose it, and everyday thereafter take steps towards achieving it.

A vision board is not a bad idea and can be a collage of pictures of all the things we want our passion to represent. This board should be placed close to our sleeping quarters and at eye level so when we wake up in the morning the first thing we see are our passion and dreams.

5. **Happy and Sad moments.** We all have a special, happy moment in our life; it's the moment where we always want to tell others about this one specific occasion. Maybe it was a kid who needed a dollar at the ice cream truck and you gave him five dollars instead. This kid grew up to be a successful lawyer and you needed advice and the kid provides his services for free because you made him happy as a kid. Kids never forget moments like this and will often repay the debt because the adult took the time to care. These happy moments are great for living and spreading love with passion.

When I was in high school I lost sixty-one friends from the 9th grade to my senior year due to cancer, violence, car crashes and drugs. This was a sad part of my life, which I choose to use as a positive reinforcement to help others avoid those same situations. Now I dedicate my time to develop nonprofits and international organizations assisting underprivileged youth with educational needs.

6. **What is our legacy?** I want to leave my daughter a legacy to follow and talk about with her kids, so each day I need to

keep this in my mind that this life is not just about me but about the legacy I am trying to leave for my family. Often times we get caught up in the glitz and glam of the now but forget to leave our children with anything to build from. I do not just want to leave my daughter with bills but an idea of what living with purpose really means and the importance of enjoying life.

If I died tomorrow how would I want to be remembered by others? When following our passion we should not only think of what makes us happy, but also think of what speaks the most about our core beliefs, morals and values. When we follow our passion, we will receive fulfillment, and share this feeling with our friends and family. Passionate loving and living is a legacy in itself.

My mother and father where together for forty years and their love for one another has rubbed off on me and I am a product of their passion for each other. When we do things with passion and purpose we are building a legacy for all the children in our family to follow and replicate. One of my biggest passions is cheering for the Dallas Cowboys every Sunday with my daughter screaming, "go Dallas go Dallas go" and to now hear her repeat those words without force from me is awesome.

B. PURSUE HAPPINESS

1. **Develop resources.** Now that we have figured out what we want now we need to determine what is needed to make our goals a reality. We need to tap into our resources and get the ball rolling on our objectives. We need to record all of the things on our to-do list, which means we may need external assistance. Developing our resources means we will create a list of people who have already been where we

are trying to go. If we are interested in running for governor we will partner up with previous governors and learn the ropes of the business. This is a list of internal resources we can tap into at any given time to make sure we are headed in the right direction.

In the pursuit of passion, we cannot be afraid to ask for help, admit to wrongdoing, and admit that we do not know something. The fulfillment comes in the end from this exertion of energy. According to Paula Rizzo there are five health benefits from making a list: reduces our anxiety or fear, boosting our brainpower, improving our focus, increasing self-esteem, and organizing our thoughts. All of these benefits will help us feel well about finding and pursuing our passion by just writing a list of people we can call and ask questions.

2. **Make a poster of our daily thoughts.** Similar to a vision board, but different in the fact that we want your poster to be from social media, magazines and other reading documents. This means we want to capture everything we come across in our daily activity that represents our vision. Then break the poster into three sections titled: the things I love to do, the things I want to do, and the things I just do.

    The goal will be to do more things we love to do and want to do and reduce the amount of things we just do. This poster will also be a helpful addition to complement our vision board. The pictures should be the same as the pictures on the vision board. If we go back and carefully trace our happiness, we will begin to see things are interconnected.

3. **Listening to Intuition.** This is one of the most powerful rules in my life, which I have a hard time following

sometimes. If I would have only listened to my gut when I was younger I may have been the president of the US.

Listening to our gut can save us a lot of heartache and pain. We must learn to listen to our instincts; most of the time we make impulse decisions based on emotional feelings and previous experiences. We have to learn how to control our emotions and focus on making a sound decision for the better good. My favorite saying is, "Listen to your gut or you will end up on your butt."

To me, intuition is when we know or sense something without being able to explain how we came to that conclusion rationally. It is the mysterious gut feeling or instinct that often turns out to be right in retrospect. This is where prayer and faith play a big role in the decision making process. We need to have a strong belief in God, this will help us get through the tough times and have faith to hold on.

Faith gives us enough time to make it until help arrives, a lucky break happens or our competition falls and it's our time to step up. If the faith inside us is strong and well-nourished we will know when something or someone is not good for us. This is not a relationship book but this is a book to help us think, live and walk in the right direction. Faith will build strength within us to make the right decision and live a purposeful life.

4. **Create a passion plan.** Now that we have an idea of what our passion is, it's time to create a plan. But before we do anything, we will need to gather all the information we have thus far (goals, objective, poster and vision board). This does not have to be very fancy; it can be a simple list of what we plan to do, when and where. Once we finish writing the plan, we will need to share the plan with

someone else and we will ask this person to be the Project Manager of our passion.

This person will be responsible for keeping us on time, schedule and below cost. I have achieved my success in life because I always had a plan and I was very flexible to updating my plan with new ideas and concepts. Now we have someone who is passionate as well. The person selected should pay attention to details and will not be afraid to challenge our plan. This will give us a better understanding of the feasibility of our plan and if it needs revisions.

5. **Find a mentor.** Mentors are critical to helping us find our way. I would ask a friend, colleague or professor about a worthy person to mentor you on our journey. We will need mentors in our passion, faith and our personal life to help keep us focused on our end goal. These three mentors or maybe one can satisfy all our requirements. If the field is completely new, find two or three passionpreneurs that have achieved success and discuss with them what it takes to achieve success. For me, finding someone with the same passion is vital to my development and maturity in my craft.

When I decided to write, I did not consult with my friend who hated reading, I consulted a published author. Life is 90% planning! How I wish I knew this before I took my SAT exam, but we live and learn. If we are prepared for the hurdles to come, we are more likely to be successful because, again," if we can see it we can do it!"

Think as if we are Olympic hurdlers and we have two hurdles races to complete. The first race we have clear weather and we can see the finish line and the things we need to do to finish what we started. The next race is under foggy conditions and the hurdles can only be seen when we are actually close up on them, preventing us from running our fastest because we do not know where the hurdles are and we try to prevent all of our falls. The first race is the equivalent of having a mentor; someone who has been through the same process we are undergoing and has the foresight to guide us mentally to the finish line and then second race is finishing the race without a mentor.

We will come across problems along the way that may cloud our thinking and not having a person to call and ask questions will discourage us from finishing our task. The addition of a mentor helps us: work smarter not harder, gain access to resources, navigate trouble waters, clarify our plan, provide different perspectives, identify potential gaps, recognize unknown opportunities, achieve measurable successes, develop, and network.

6. **Believe in self**. One of the most confusing things in life comes in the form of the love and protection of our family and friends. They want us to be successful (there is no doubt), but they often will answer questions about our life based on the experiences within their life, which not be the best answer at the time. The reality is we are all built differently and what happened to them may not happen to us.

We will come into contact with friends, parents, counselors, and colleagues who will tell us, "No don't quit your good job; no don't do it! You will fail at following your dreams!" This is not all true. The same people that doubted or were scared for our failure will be basking and bathing in our success. Think of yourself as a point guard and there are twenty seconds left on the clock and we are winning by one point. Now the logical thing would be to run the clock out or let the team foul you, but instead you decide to shoot the ball from the three-point line and the coach yells, "No!!!" Then the ball goes in and the coach yells great shot. Passion is the same way, if we are successful everyone says great job but if we quit or fail, everyone will say, "I told you so". This is what our peers will do. If we don't believe in our passion, why should anybody else? I just brushed those types of people off and love them from afar.

C. MANAGE LIFE

1. **Get feedback.** The majority of stars who reach greatness have always thought of how to get there and what to with the wealth once they obtain it, but very few have thought about the day they stop working. This is the reason for multiple athletes and entertainers losing everything, poor management of life after finding their passion.

   It takes a great deal of training, focus and energy to find our passion and then get good at it but once we acquire it we cannot forget about the future. Time to look outside of our own perspective and consult with close friends to get their feedback on our spending, time management, leisure activities and spirit. Sometimes we are so submerged in ourselves that we forget to analyze ourselves.

   Others close to us will provide constructive criticism to help us stay focused and disciplined in our approach to finding purpose. Have our moods changed? Are we more energetic, reliable and still driven? In our circle of friends we need people who have the courage to tell us the truth instead of letting us continuously make the same mistakes. These friendships are instrumental to developing not only us but also the trust in others and valuing each other's opinion. Benefits to feedback include the ability to correct a mistake without making it continuous, learn a new skill quickly as possible, and improve our current skill sets. My belief is constructive criticism involves construction of self, building trust, self-esteem, listening skills and the ability to pay attention to details. The quickest way to building new technology is listening to our customer base versus listening to our own wants and needs.

2. **Practice.** Just because we find our passion does not mean we stop working to improve it or skill set. In fact if it is something we love to do, practice will not seem that bad, it gives a chance to perfect our skills and show the world what we are truly made of.

A pianist will practice the same song countless hours over and over again until it becomes muscles memory, like a pure shooter in the NBA. Think of Seth Curry who is currently one of the best shooters of all time. Every time Mr. Curry takes a jump shot it is with the same mechanics and form no matter stress or external circumstances. It is as if he slows time down just to get in the perfect motion to flick his wrist and fire away. It will be the same for you once you find and continuously practice your passion, muscle memory.

Once I obtain something I am passionate about, I practiced it over and over again until it becomes muscle memory and then I would prepare myself for the moment I needed to showcase my talents. It is the practice which makes us perfect, we learn our weakness, strengths and things we can change to improve our craft (For details see my eBook on *"Mastering Your Craft"*, Dec 2014 Amazon, Nook & Create space).

Without practice we are merely free styling or alibiing our way through our passion, but we always have to remember there is always someone out there with the same dreams and working as hard as us or harder. Like Mr. Curry we should practice our craft over and over again building our confidence and self-esteem. Practice is important because it prepares us for the test.

The thing about life is we know test are coming in our relationships, work, and mental mainframe but no one knows the date of the test. In college we could prepare for the test, study and determine the structure of the test but not in real life. Anything can happen at any time in real life and as practice prepares us for these types of situations, we will always be ready.

Throughout my life my biggest rewards have happened when I least expected it and somehow I was prepared from a previous lesson. The old saying practice makes perfect is correct! I would rephrase it to say practice makes muscle memory! THAT makes us perfect via practice.

3. **Invest in self.** The first investment we should make is in ourselves. We tend to invest our time, thought, and energy into everything else but ourselves sometimes but we must have discipline to pull ourselves back and focus on reinvesting in ourselves. The best investment I made in my life is investing into my own dreams and admirations.

In life we might have multiple passions at one time (Ex: Passion for religion, career and love life) but with planning and prioritizing our work and personal life balance we can do the same for our passion. My mentor Dr. Charles Glass once said, "You have three great ideas, which one are you going to give 100% to? Currently you are giving 33.3% percent to three good ideas, but when will you make your ideas great?" He wanted me to finish all three projects but just one at a time, which is fully invested. I followed his lead and completed this book.

Sometimes we focus on looking busy instead of having a legitimate reason for being busy. In order to get others to invest in our ideas we must fully invest in ourselves. An investor is more likely to invest in someone who is passionate and invested in himself or herself, versus a person who just has a fancy business plan. Put your money where your passion is.

4. **Positive thinking at all times.** Keeping a circle of positive people around you at all times is very important to thinking positive and looking on the bright side of all situations. You have to build a force field to repel negative thinking and energy, which are distractions from your passion and purpose.

    According to Elizabeth Scott the optimists explained, "Positive events as having happened because of themselves, they also see them as evidence that more positive things will happen in the future (stable), and in other areas of their lives (global). Conversely, they see negative events as not being their fault (external). They also see them as being flukes (isolated) that have nothing to do with other areas of their lives or future events (local) versus a pessimist who thinks in the opposite way. Pessimists believe they cause negative events themselves (internal). They believe that one mistake means more will come (stable), and mistakes in other areas of life are inevitable (global), because they are the cause. They see positive events as flukes (local) that are caused by things outside their control (external) and probably won't happen again (unstable)."

Some key principles I use for staying positive are the following: find the silver lining (there is always a message in everything we do), find the positive energy from the message, and learn from the negative. Gratitude is the best way to move forward. Be grateful for everything on your journey, keep your head up and heart open; life will not be easy but you are built for the journey. Know that bad days will eventually become good, and make notes of the positive message you hear each day.

The goal is to be a positive water hose spraying water all throughout the community to help passion seeds grow, not to be a passion sponge just absorbing passion but very little spreading of it. Positive people bring about new ideas and opportunity because they think and live freely without the fear of stress.

D. DO BETTER

1. **Share.** Once we have searched for our passion, pursued it and now we have received it, the time has come to be it! Show the world who you are and what you're passionate about. If we have not received a monetary reward by now, during this phase is where we will discover it; the key is to stay focused and committed to our craft.

The most beneficial part of life is the ability to give back to others. God has blessed you with the opportunity to follow your dreams; so, I would suggest repaying him by showing someone else how to follow their passion. Once we have been through the fire and survived we should turn back and not turn our back on the community.

If we all reinvested in the community where we developed, it would make the world a better place. Giving back is the key to moving up in our career and living a life of fulfillment. Giving back does not have to be only monetary, there are other ways to increase the living, learning and developing opportunities in our communities.

A major role of a passionpreneur is to be a passion angel for someone else while working within his or her own passion. We should spend quality time each day showing gratitude for the blessings we have. There is someone out there with the same question we had before and we would be the perfect person to answer it. Give back today.

Do it *pro bono* or for little to nothing at first. Volunteering is key to developing and discovering our passion. I found my passion for coaching and mentoring by giving of my time and efforts to people for free and the reward was far greater. The friendship, community enrichment, turning boys to productive men, and self-fulfillment is priceless. Merrill and associate created an article on volunteering and the benefits are: we will learn or develop a new skill, be a part of the community, be motivated internally and have a s sense of achievement, be subjected to new opportunities, develop new hobbies and interest, new experiences, meet diverse ranges of people and send a message to our friend circle about positivity.

Volunteering is crucial to the full development of your passion and you must stay in touch with the community in which you are developing your passion. Each time we step out and do things we meet new people, who become new friends and potentially new customers.

2. **Travel more.** Often times, the accomplishments and setbacks absorb us; this box will mentally handicap us to the things happening in our immediate world. To understand our potential, we need to get the perspective of

others outside our social circle of family members and friends. This will give us a holistic look into our passion and places us in position to become an expert, because we will bring a new perspective to the table.

We live in a country full of diversity from Capitol Hill to the countryside in Texas, the United States has become a very multicultural place to live and raise a family. Traveling will help us get a better understanding of how blessed we are and keep us humble for success. See the world and bring back valuable lessons learned, new cultures and similarities between cultures. This comparison from our existing world versus the world we explore during our travel will broaden our horizon and open our eyes to new opportunities.

The world is full of passionpreneurs, now we just need to find them to spread the love. When traveling, I pay respect to the values and beliefs of the locals I meet, and I do not bestow my judgment on their way of living. Just listen and learn.

3. **Smile more!** Smiling in pain is the key to getting through painful times. Smiling has sealed the deal on business meetings for me and helped me mentally motivate others who were not having a good day. When we are having a rough day, as the 1984 Gillette Company TV commercial slogan said, "Never let them see you sweat!" Smiling will take us to the top; it is a self-discipline exercise we can use to help us retain our composure.

I remember walking to class at Howard University and being approached by two gunmen from the local neighborhood screaming, "Give me all you got". I then gladly handed over my wallet with nothing in it and my metro card but I was smiling through the entire ordeal and never said a word. One of the young men said, "Man he crazy, he been smiling the entire time". The men called me mentally retarded, shock their heads, and walked away, I just kept smiling and picked up my wallet.

Smiling helped me control my emotions and conceal my true feelings of anger and aggression. Following our passion comes with stress, drama, and bad days. But we can face these negative events with positive energy and a smile. A smile is a powerful tool. Once we utilize it the correct way, it will reduce our stress and helps us build confidence within ourselves.

4. **We are blessed**! There are people who rarely get the opportunity to have an opportunity, so if we have the blessing to be able to follow our dreams and make them a reality, we are highly favored and blessed. There have been people before and after us who will never get the opportunity to follow their dreams and for this fact we must appreciate the opportunity.

    With blessings comes big responsibility. One major responsibility will be how well we manage our work and personal life. This is not an easy fix but with communication, preparation and common sense, we can make sensible decisions and spend quality time with our career and family. Passionpreneurs do not mind working long hours -we love the work - but there is more to life than our jobs.

    I recommend the following priority list: God first, family second, and career third. Life is too short to spend an eternity focusing on the work instead of developing a strong relationship with God and nurturing our family bonds. Death is eminent in life and if we spend quality time with our family we are considered successful in my book.

I always see movie stars, comedians, and politicians taking leave of absence to spend more time with their family, because their work totally consumes them, it's their passion. But they also have a passion for their family and a decision has to be made as kids and grandparents get older. We have to cherish the time we have with our passion but also remember our loved ones who have helped us reach our destination. I wish there was a time machine to go back and replay our lives, but as of today that has not been created, so love the family you have.

FAILURE IS NOT AN OPTION
"Embrace opportunities to be with empathetic people. You'll likely walk away from your time with them feeling warmly embraced in return"

Failure is nothing to be afraid of. It is to be recognized, learned from and used as a motivational tool to enhance our productivity. We should be ready to face rejection and fear of failing, because it is always a preliminary to most successful events. Failure is part of success. I have failed more times in life than I succeeded, but my failures taught me how to succeed. They prepared me to be successful.

In Chapter six I will share real life stories from various superstars who have faced failure but managed to keep going and now are leaders of the world in their respective craft. Failure propels us forward and builds our confidence so we can lead others to their passion.

Trying to write a book is difficult but fifteen years prior to this year I poorly wrote minutes for a scientific committee and I submitted my subpar work for my supervisor to critique and she was so upset with me that I thought she was going to fire me. I will never forget that day; because it was the moment I truly learned how to capture notes, transfer them into content and how to write. She challenged me to shape up or ship out and I decided to shape up. I have to admit my fear in high school turned out to be my strength when I became an adult. I feared running; now I run marathons. I hated working out; now I work out four days a week, and I hated reading, but now read six books a month and I'm writing my own books. Facing our fears equals finding our passion.

Let me tell a story about how I got into motivational speaking. As a kid my parents forced me to give presentations, say the family prayers, speaking in the public and the list goes on and on. I was trained to be respectful but they unknowingly and subliminally trained me to be a motivational speaker. I remember my first time going to Bible study, and the elders asked me to read the Bible in front of the class. My world stopped and I was in a state of pure shock. What would happen if I pronounced a word wrong? This was pure fear for a twelve year old, but I managed to get through the reading. The reading was not as bad as it seemed and I faced my fear and won.

Arina Nikitina, listed the following steps for overcoming our fears, I have added my two scents after each topic:

1. **Take action.** To overcome fear, we must act and act boldly with confidence. Actions will give us a chance to change the circumstances. Passionpreneurs believe actions speak louder than words. When fear presents itself in our life, do not run away from it; run towards it and let our actions speak for us. I was afraid of flying in an airplane but I faced my fear by learning about the safety of flying and now you cannot keep me off a plane.

2. **Be persistent.** Successful people don't give up. They will

keep trying every option possible until the task is satisfied. Unsuccessful people will try one time and quit. In our journey we will be denied, laughed at, and rejected, but that is okay because we believe in ourselves and will push pass the distractions. The word quit does not exist in our vocabulary. Passionpreneurs will never quit; it is just not in our character.

3. **Do things differently.** There is an old saying, "If you always do what you've always done, you'll always get what you already got". If we are not getting the results we want, then we should do something different. When I was younger and hanging with the wrong people, I was getting the wrong results, and I began to get frustrated and tired, so I had to change my actions and surroundings. This change helped me graduate college and graduate school. To change our outputs, we have to change our inputs.

4. **Do not be too hard on yourself and do not take failure personally**. Failure is about behavior, outcomes, and results. Just because we make mistakes does not mean that we failed. Do not be too hard on yourself; the world is very good at doing that. We are our worst critics most times, and understand mistakes are a part of life. Face our fears and we will be one step closer to our destiny.

I was volunteering as a coach for a youth organization and I made a bad-coaching decision in the final minutes of the basketball game that caused my team to lose the game. I took the loss personally and I did not have a chance to get my team ready for the next game. My team came out sluggish and carried the attitude from the previous game. I understood at that moment people depended on me and failing was bigger than myself; I needed to learn how to forget a loss so that the performance in the game prior would not resurface.

We must teach ourselves to grieve but grieve while getting up. Hard days will come and we must plan for those days; we must learn how to not get depressed over stress. If we lose, we have an excellent opportunity to teach and learn from our mistakes. Stay positive during a loss and we will always gain something in return.

5. **Treat the experience as an opportunity to learn.** Think of failure as a learning experience. Ask the following questions. What was the mistake? Why did it happen? How could it have been prevented? How can I do better next time? Life is a learning experience; we must learn to forgive and ask for forgiveness. Life is too short to hold grudges and negative emotions while trying to pursue your passion; it will be a distraction. Learning is essential to building and sustaining our right frame of mind.

6. **Look for possible opportunities from any experience.** Bad experiences are an opportunity to create a good experience. Every bad situation in my life proved later to be a blessing in disguise. Find the silver lining in the mistakes you make in your relationships, career, and personal life. When we least expect things to happen that's when they will happen.

7. **Fail forward fast.** Meaning if we want to learn faster, we must fail faster and learn from that failure, the management guru. The best example of this is the National Football League's New England Patriots football team; this football coaching staff takes the mistakes made in the first half and uses them as learning tools for the next half of play.

It is amazing to see someone rise from defeat and apply it to his or her life, resulting in instant progress. I did the same thing for my life. The mistakes I made along the way helped me learn my lessons the hard way and led me to a better place as I aged and matured. I look back to acknowledge the path I had taken to get to where I am, but I did not look back to repeat the same steps, because I had learned from my mistakes and made them my strengths

Message from this chapter: *Make a firm decision to understand you are more than enough to make your dreams come true and deserve to be happy. Don't failure to hard and learn from your mistakes by being open and honest with yourself.*

-SECTION II: FUEL-
Something moves you. What is it?

CHAPTER 3: MAXIMIZING PASSION

TESTIMONY: SEXUAL ASSAULT SURVIVOR

Now that we have a sense of direction, we need to maximize our potential and continue to build our passion and skills, which will help keep our passion alive. Every day we witness people all over the world showing heroic efforts of passion with purpose, from the weather in the Philippines to the airplane 370 gone missing from Malaysia. People care about people. In this chapter we want to discuss steps to maximize our passion and get the most out of our dreams.

When I was in my twenties and extremely excited about becoming of age, being able to feel like an adult, free of the shackles of my parents and pursuing independence through a college degree, I had the opportunity to meet Kristina Gilchrist a very vibrant and cute young lady with a smile to melt any heart. Little did I know my friend was living in a world of turmoil and instability. Only fifteen years into our friendship did I know she was raised in a drug infested home, crack houses and drug dealers everywhere often feeling the role of family member while her dad proceeded to get high.

This bright and intelligent young lady did not let her environment stop her from reaching her fullest potential. At the age of 10 years old she began shopping on her own, often catching a cab downtown D.C. to shop amongst the who's who and browse the scenery. Mentally accepting her reality, not quitting, embracing the love and support from her grandmother and other friends she gained along the way.

Though her father was addicted to drugs, he did provide a positive role model to Mrs. Gilchrist when he was sober. Drugs were not the only battle Mrs. Gilchrist had to endure, attempted sexual assault by her cousin at 8 years old, raped by a neighborhood "play brother"/friend while sleeping and threatened to be set ablaze by her attacker. All of this did not stop this passion pioneer from becoming the gems she is today.

Mrs. Gilchrist has taken her pain and created love within her community by developing a book and workbook for victims who have been sexually assaulted, spoken at various youth/adult conferences, served as a workshop guest speaker, and helped create programs in Washington, D.C. to support the development of young men and women where she was raised.

She could have walked away from the city, which took so much from her, but she did not, she stood up and faced her fear and created a family with passion and love, then she shared her story with others to help prevent them from making the same mistakes or putting themselves in vulnerable positions.

This book is dedicated to people who have been through things and somehow mustered the strength and energy to overcome adversity with passion and purpose. If you want more information about Mrs. Gilchrist go visit at www.csjirstiangilcrest.com, she will embrace you with open arms.

"If hostility passes through my camp that is one thing. But if it puts down stakes in my camp, I must either exercise my right to move away from it or accept my responsibility to address it"

ACCEPTING ADVERSITY

Adversity is a part of everyday living no matter how old we are. It's a part of everyone's journey. We have to move forward with the fruit of passion when we are faced with adversity and understand that our purpose is much bigger than the adversity we are facing. We have no inclination what the future holds and we should have faith in the adversity, as it will be for the better good of our growth and development.

When we stand up against adversity, we may not win the

war, but we may win the battle by gaining confidence in our strength (do not quit mentally). On the other hand, if we run (flight), we may regain security, but we will have to face the same fear again. Facing our fears will reduce our tears in the long term.

Adversity to me is a doorknob we have to turn in order to open the door to reach our full potential. When we are faced with adversity big or small we should tell ourselves "I will never quit. I will work with what I have; and I will remain positive at all times". This is a winning mindset. To help us through adversity, we must keep our eyes on our goals, which will reassure us we are focused.

Next, stay as close to positive people as we possibly can. Positive people have a way of thinking under pressure and being concise with decision-making. If we have a problem there needs to be a friend whom we can contact to help us get through adversity. I personally like calling upon my faith. The goal is to keep our circle of friends as drama and stress free as possible.

Understand the origin of the adversity, lesson learned from it and how we could handle the situation the next time it occurs.

When we are facing adversity it is a wise move to talk with our mentor or advisor. Talking with someone who has been in our shoes before can help us make better decisions and help us when we face adversity. A man's new best friend is the "navigation system" in his vehicle; it can guide him in the right direction and if he goes in the wrong direction, he can blame the navigation system. Mentors are helpful walking navigation system for both men and women, leading us both in the right direction to live a passionate and purposeful life.

Prayer is also helpful, because it provides a level of comfort when we are faced with adversity, it reaffirms everything will be okay. Prayer can go a long way to help us get up and over any adversity we are facing. We have to get into the habit of taking time out of every day to reflect on the important things in life. I utilize different forms of meditation to help me relax whether it is yoga, reading, Zumba or listening to music. Whatever it takes to clear our mind and get us completely relaxed is what we need to do.

The quiet times of meditation and self-enrichment help me refocus, then realign my priorities and finally confirm I am on the right path. We are continuously beat up by society and need to give our mind, body and soul some time to heal from the beating, take the time to rest from the stress. Adversity is real, but if we keep a positive attitude towards adversity, the damage will be manageable and minimal at best.

PASSION MAYBE UNCOMFORTABLE

A wise professor once told me, "get comfortable being uncomfortable Mr. Hill" while I was in the middle of my presentation on why Howard University was my college of choice. Though he was specifically talking about getting comfortable being uncomfortable speaking in front of my peers, his words resonated throughout my life.

I really cannot remember the last time I was 100% comfortable, I have a life with comfort in it but to say my life is a piece of cake without work is fantasy that will never happen. I work tirelessly to improve and polish my skills to make sure I am ready when the phone rings. Living a life of passion means we may do things that may not be comfortable in nature, for example long hours, and studying all night.

Doing the things we have less comfort in doing can build our comfort level in those situations. For instance, if I do not like dogs and then I am placed in a situation where I am forced to be around dogs, I might then begin to learn how to tolerate or maybe love dogs, my un-comfort zone (fear) has become a comfort zone (confidence).

According to Webster's dictionary ***the comfort zone is*** the level at which a person functions with ease and familiarity. A comfort zone is a stress-less place! Yes, we must breach the comfort zone and move our lives over to the uncomfortable zone.

Once we achieve happiness life gets comfortable but it will never be perfectly comfortable. Life is continuously evolving and change is eminent. The best person to be around is the person who enjoys being uncomfortable; they don't run away from what is not familiar to them. Being able to function outside of your comfort zone shows courage, faith and flexibility. My comfort zone hindered me a few times in life but I refused to let it stop me from my purpose.

> *"Faith does not eliminate questions, but faith knows where to take them."* -**Elisabeth Elliot**

To leave my comfort zone, I began traveling to speak with kids all over the world for free about their dreams and wishes. Their love for me helped me find my passion for writing and getting the word of passion out to everyone. Kids have an innocent way of asking every question and laughing through adversity.

When we get to adulthood we tend to over- and under-think actions before they happen. I was uncomfortable speaking about my real life stories because I did not think much of them, I thought my story was the same as others but to these kids my story was a success story full of ups and downs but I made it to success. A kid that has very little opportunity will indulge in our stories because they are searching for a way out of their life situations. The kids helped me gain confidence in sharing my stories, beliefs, and values to the world.

We must get over the opinion of others and focus on the opinions we have inside of ourselves. Passion is not given; it is worked for and chased. When following our dreams, we have to first THINK then we have to think outside of the box. Get accustomed to being uncomfortable to find passion and success. I spent countless hours reading and writing, researching my competition, got rid of toxic relationships, refused phone calls and isolated myself from the world to pursue my dreams. Nothing was going to stop me from using imagination, increasing my innovation and instilling my motivation upon others.

FIGHTING FIRE WITH WATER

This section is very dear to me. For some reason I could not understand this concept, until I was older: we cannot fight fire with fire. As a kid in Prince Georges County Maryland, I grew up with the mindset of "If someone does something to us, we were going to do something to you". As an adult, this way of thinking will send us a "go to jail" card, so I changed my way of thinking before I became a functioning adult.

If we want to keep the fire going, we should fight fire with fire, but if we want to eliminate the fire we should look to provide a solution that will smother the life of the fire, simply add water. I call this one the "losing the battle but winning the war" methodology. Life is not always about winning. Sometimes it is about surviving until the next adversity or opportunity.

Too often our pride gets in the way when we hear the words retreat, loss, lose, weakness, fear, walk away, turn the other cheek or afraid, but within these words lies a great opportunity for power.

I remember seeing a high-school friend in an argument over a young lady and fists were soon to fly. I told him to walk away. He resisted and began to ball up his fist, plotting his assault. I simply told him. "If you punch him, you will be punching me, and then you are fighting for a lost cause. Thank him and walk away." Something clicked in his mind and the young man walked away. He is no longer dating the young lady and his friend has since stopped talking to the young lady because she did the same thing to him. Eventually, the two young men forgave each other and remained friends.

Let's say he did punch him and they fought. This would lead to an ongoing feud and we never know what this disagreement would escalate to. Learn to walk away from drama and walk into your purpose. Passion takes discipline and we will be tested along the way. When we are faced with drama, we have to exercise discipline and self-control to walk away and turn the other cheek. Walking away is temporarily giving up power, but in the end we will regain the power lost because we applied self-discipline and maturity to defuse the situation.

In sports, successful teams consistently are the teams that develop a thorough game plan and stick to it no matter what their opposition is trying to force them to do. Teams will not be successful if they play according to the other team's game plan. My favorite NFL team, the Dallas Cowboys, has a powerful running game; it is their "bread and butter". One game in the 2013-14 season, they faced quarterback Peyton Manning and the red hot Denver Broncos, the best passing team in the NFL this particular year. For Dallas to have a chance to win they could not fight fire with fire; they had to stick to their game plan and execute.

Once we set our game plan for the day, we need to stay away from distractions which are trying to satisfy their own game plan and do not really care about our wellbeing. We need to develop a game plan, stick to it, and make adjustments if necessary to adjust to the activities of now. It is one thing to have a plan, but it is another skill to be able to adjust on the fly. Based on their record, Dallas was a weaker passing team, but a strong running team. Stick to the plan and we can compete with anyone. To keep the fire burning add fire, to diffuse the fire add water.

TURN FEAR INTO STRENGTH

"If I allow fear to dictate my actions/my next move, I will always

*be reacting to imagined life rather than responding to my real one." –***Oumar Hill**

Fear needs to be faced with confidence, boldness and conviction, and this will convert our weaknesses to strengths. Growing up in a sports family, we got trained in the art of turning the adrenaline or fear into the passion. My first sign of fear that I experienced at twelve years old was better known as "butterflies" in my stomach. This feeling would only come around during rivalry games; my adrenaline was at an all-time high.

Some ran from the challenge but I loved to face my fears, it was the rush of the fear of not knowing what would happen. The hours of practice and preparation prepared me mentally for my competition and the opportunity to compete was a blessing. I understand fear is a part of nature, but we can transform this fear into motivation to overcome any obstacle in our life. We just have to defeat one fear and then the other fears we have in life will be less effective on our psyche. If a fighter gets caught with a good punch that knocks him down, how many times will he get up? Fear may keep him down, but determination and perseverance will help him get up and recover from being knocked down.

Once we learn how to live with faith, passion and perseverance, we will reduce the fear we have for things in our life. The following techniques are helpful for changing your fear into faith:

1. Prior to transforming Fear
    a. Thank God
    b. Have faith
    c. Know our weaknesses
    d. Know the steps needed to be successful
    e. Know what causes you to fail
    f. Practice developing your strengths

g. I there are teammates involved, study them and help them improve

2. During the transformation
   a. Stay humble
   b. Follow the plan
   c. Be willing to make adjustments
   d. Never give up
   e. Positive Self-talk
   f. Talk yourself through positively
   g. Stay focused on your goal

3. Transformation completion
   a. Forget your fears quickly
   b. Learn from your mistakes
   c. Celebrate competing
   d. Always leave room for improvement
   e. Okay to be wrong
   f. Fall down with dignity, get up with purpose
   g. Be grateful

ASSOCIATE WITH WHO YOU WANT TO BECOME

To find and keep our passion, we need to associate with people of like character and mindset. Success has a price and we must be prepared to sacrifice some things. Success is not easy and we cannot take everyone with us. Sacrifice takes discipline, acceptance, and hours upon hours of hard work and determination.

If the people in our lives are not of like mind, then we need to remove ourselves and allow them to handle their own personal drama. There is only one Dr. Phil and we need to focus on how to be ourselves and preform at a high level. We are all human and mistakes are unpreventable, but if we are prepared for mistakes we can limit the damages.

The world loves passionate people for two reasons: to see them rise and to see them fall. If we fall, be prepared for the solitude, ridicule, and disembowelment of our character and the people around us. But once we hang or associate with people who have already been where we are trying to go, we can gain some foresight and hindsight from their experience and convert it to the steps we are taking in our lives.

There is nothing wrong with hanging with people that we love, but when it comes to passion, we have to make sure those individuals are of the same mindset, if not they will become a handicap and will hold us back. This does not mean they have to think or act like us, but they have to understand sacrificing Friday and Saturday social events, happy hour ventures may have to stop, or excessive shopping may have to stop. In addition, these individuals around us have to be aware of our thought process and cannot bombard us with dramatic and stressful discussions about negativity because it will change our focus.

"Know when to tell family members and friends, I love you but you need counseling. Your problems are higher than my pay grade. I am sorry in advance."
-Oumar Hill

To be successful we must be willing to transform the criticism and negative energy to persevere and share our ideas with the world. Our life is meant to be a living testimony for others to learn from and utilize as a template for their own life. We are natural creators of innovation and challengers of the normalcies of life. Our goal is to make the world a better place, make people wiser, and foster better relationships amongst the diverse ethnicities in the world. On the road to following our passion, negative people will be magnetically attracted to us and will try to distract us from our purpose. But if we follow the rules in this book, we will avoid setbacks and detours.

There is a short window to define what and who we want to become. Once we make the decision, we must remain focused and learn quickly. To help us navigate, here are a few characteristics of negative people:

1. Play the victim
2. Controlling
3. Frequently Gossip
4. Excessively complains
5. Passively listens
6. Not focused on a solution
7. Narrow minded
8. Crying Wolf
9. Jealous
10. Insecure

Negative people need attention and this attention will distract us from our destination. We have to decide are we the neighborhood shrink or are we living with passion. Negative people will slow us down from achieving our goals and may prevent us from achieving them, if we let them. They are not purposefully bad people; maybe they fell on hard times and need time to readjust. We have to be mindful and careful with whom we associate with today because it will show tomorrow. We are who we associate with and we must be selective in real life and online with the increase of social media.

MANAGE DISTRACTIONS
"But I tell you not to resist an evil person. But whoever slaps you on your right cheek, turn the other to him also."
-Matthew 5:39

We should carefully review the people who are currently in our lives. Think of our lives as a bank account and we need to monitor the deposits and withdrawals people utilize each day. This will be helpful to determine our real friends versus conditional friends. True friends will deposit more into us instead of taking from us. On the other hand, conditional friends are only around for specific conditions and if the conditions are not upheld they will not remain a friend.

On the road to following our passion, our discipline will be tested daily but we must remain strong and purpose driven! Once we live the right way we will not only attract passionate people, but we will also attract "passion sponges". Think of the one family member who complains about everything and life has always not been fair. In addition, some individuals are looking for ideas to steal. They will disguise themselves as friends to win over our friendship. These people often suffer from lack of discipline and motivation, as well as self-esteem and communication issues. They are modern day vampires waiting to claim our passion blood but with hard work and faith we will be too authentic to copy.

Now, passion sponges are very evasive and manipulative. As we are searching for our dreams we must keep our eye on the prize and weed out the negative people and passion sponges. Just because we have found our passion, it does not mean we will not stop the distraction or the drama. Knowing this, we must increase our self-discipline and self-actualization to sustain our passion.

Protect our passion and minds with our lives. When we are on a mission to follow our dreams we must give up our old ways and ride off into the sunset. WE CANNOT SAVE EVERYONE. Listed below are a few key points to reduce fear:

"Positive thinking is the key to finding, securing, and sustaining your passion."
-**Oumar Hill**

1. **Fear of our own failure.** We spend too much time anticipating failure and often this leads to our ultimate failure. We do not have time to invest our thoughts into negative ideas. We need to focus 100% of our energy into positive things only. We have to focus on not being a distraction but an addition.

    Compliment the process and build on what we already have in a friendship or relationship. We cannot take away more than we have given. We get in our own way sometimes because of fear and convince ourselves this will never happen and we don't deserve it. Leave fear at home and go chase your dreams.

    Fear of failure comes in many forms like uncertainty, upsetting others or not valuing our worth. To get over our fears we should learn how to control our emotions and thoughts, life is too short and we need to cherish every moment.

2. **Social media is addictive.** If not managed wisely social media can encompass our entire day, mind and life. If managed correctly, social media can help us share our passion with the world in a timely and cost effective manner.

    With the explosion of social media and the Internet growing into a community of its own, we must learn when to put the computer down and lift ourselves up. I remember the day when I only used the Internet to look at email. Now I need it to upload my Instagram pictures, manage my financial accounts, update my family and friends

(Facebook), and read the news (twitter). The Internet can methodically place our lives in a box - the box of no return! Be mindful of the time we spend online.

3. **Stay away from passion vampires.** These individuals have a negative story every time we encounter them. "My car got towed." "I lost my job." "My rent is overdue." "I'm getting old." The list goes on and on. They are the opposite of a passionpreneur. Instead of trying to find the good in everything, they look for the bad. There is no need for negative energy in our circle. My motto is "No drama and little stress will keep me blessed".

4. **Get out of our own way.** Sometimes we are our biggest hurdles we have to face in our life. We need to step out of our comfort zone and expect more for ourselves.

    Getting out of our own way, means to go forward with your goals and refrain from being distracted and letting fear discourage progress. This may take some self-reflection because we can become naïve to some of the hurdles in our life preventing us from achieving greatness.

5. **Backsliding.** I have to admit I am not perfect by any means, no matter how I seem to be, I am a human and I enjoy being one. In following our dreams I stated we must have discipline, stay away from drama, negative relationships and people and stay focused. But we all know, we don't always listen to advice given, Think of a person we were in a relationship or business deal with that we should not have been with and everyone said be careful. Curiosity is just a human trait, which we often have to satisfy to cure. So we don't have to be perfect but we must be able to stop the backsliding. People utilize this word

when fellow Christians have fallen back into a life of sin. We will use it very similar in nature but our focus will cover more than just sin. Anything which does not serve our purpose with passion is considered a tool to push us towards backsliding and we need to work towards preventing this by doing the following things:

1. Remember who we are and what we are trying to accomplish
2. Let go and let God
3. Digress and do the work
4. Renew your faith in self
5. Define why we backslide
6. Meditate on positive vibes
7. Thank God for the lesson
8. Stop the activities of backsliding
9. Refocus on the plan
10. Define meaning of purpose in our life

Backsliding is not the end state for us, only if we do something to change the outcome. We can control our final destination by not settling for anything less than the purpose of our life and passion within our soul.

Message from this chapter: Being realistic we realize there will be adversity, distractions, bad relationships and we may have fear, but knowing this helps us manage it and maximize our potential.

CHAPTER 4: KEY FACTORS WITH-IN YOU

"The goal in life is to feel comfortable in who we are no matter where we are"
-Oumar Hill

This chapter will focus on the critical ingredients we need along the journey to reach our passion. There will be pitfalls, setbacks, and failure but we cannot quit on our dreams or ourselves. When we start the journey to following our dreams, the only way we can stop or quit is when the task is done. Growing up in Prince George's County, Maryland was not easy and temptation was always lingering nearby but someone prayed for me and I made it to my destination.

AMBITION

One of the first ingredients we need to follow our dreams is ambition. We have to have something within us, which makes us want more than the average, simultaneously pushing us to strive for greatness. Ambition will help us believe when everyone else thinks it's a bad idea or too scared to take the leap of faith.

Ambition took me to South Africa, Barbados, Canada, Ethiopia, Mexico, and other places I would have never thought of going by myself. But the key to ambition is knowing how and when to reveal our true ambition. Think of ambition as a new idea to create the next Microsoft. We have to protect our ambition until it is ready to be deployed, because if we let it out too soon, someone will try to steal the concept and/or we do not want our ambition to come back and bite us.

When we lead with ambition, we are guaranteeing we are ready to first, work harder than anyone else and second, we are determined to be successful. Passion mixed with ambition is a powerful weapon and can equip our kids to live above their dreams and not succumb to the pressures from society and peer pressure. Parents have to instill ambition in their kids to compete, survive and exceed in life.

When I think of ambition, I often reflect on rapper Wale's song *Ambition*, his lyrics spell out the true meaning of being ambitious and passionate to be successful which ties into the overarching purpose for our life. Here are some lyrics from the song, which moved me and helped me focus on my own ambition:

Intro

> The time is now, on everything
> Took my heart away from money
> I ain't interested in fame
> And I pray that never change
> Ambition is priceless
> It's something that's in your veins
> And I put that on my name

Outro

> Beautiful music, painting pictures that be my vision
> They gon love me for my ambition
> Easy to dream a dream, but much harder to live it
> Look, they gon love me for my ambition
> Beautiful music, painting pictures that be my vision
> They gon love me for my ambition

HONESTY

Let's be honest, honest is the best policy. We have to be honest with others around us and ourselves when it comes to following our passion and purpose. The only person who knows our desires and how bad we want it is ourselves, no one else. Everyone we come in contact with can interrogate us for hours and never fully comprehend the level of our desire to achieve something. We have become accustomed to hiding our true feelings, settling for less than we deserve and quitting on the process. I say this to say, we often accept the wrong path because we are too afraid of our purpose. We will settle for anyone to marry us instead of waiting for the person God has chosen for our life.

When following our passion we have to be honest with ourselves with regards to our desires, capabilities and likelihood of achieving our goal. The worst thing we can do is lie to others and ourselves, trying to live a life that satisfies others needs and not our own, this is epic failure. To follow passion, we have to love ourselves and be selfish enough to put our dreams in perspective so we can achieve them. Some situations may not allow this due to prior obligations, but this is where honesty plays a big part.

The more open and honest we are will determine the feasibility plan for making adjustments to follow our dreams. Think of honesty in the sense of a relationship. The key to a successful relationship is trust, communication and honesty. All of which play a vital role in establishing a long-term bond and relationship. I would rather a person hurt my feelings with honesty, instead of insulting our friendship with a lie.

PATIENCE

I am guilty of wanting everything now! We live in a society focused on getting everything now, instead of planting, being patient and letting things organically grow into flowers. The art of being patient is critical to follow our passion. Everything will not happen when we expect it, how we expect it and with whom we expect it. There has to be some flexibility in our timeline, scope, creep, project management, so we can maneuver things around for our long-term benefit.

When we follow our passion we are starting a new business, we are trying to figure out how this business deal will work and what are the intangible things we need to acquire to get the show on the road. It takes time to build a successful business-this involves research, commitment, and consumes a large amount of our time to fully follow our dreams. The time will pay dividends in the end, only if we put the time in and wait for our opportunity to develop. When we rush through activities we often make mistakes, overlook simple errors, and the quality of our work suffers from our unwillingness to be patient.

We have to understand there will be fast days and then there will be slow days, its called balance and once we understand this we will schedule our days around this. We will encounter some activities we can control and others we cannot. The activities we can control we can add additional resources or time to complete but the activities out of our control we have to be patient and wait for them to work themselves out. The calmness in being patient will help us reduce stress, anxiety attacks and over-thinking our solutions. Everything in our lives happens for a reason and during a season, we have to remain patient and do not focus on why we are waiting but what are we supposed to learn from waiting.

Patience was helpful for me while writing this book, when designers quit mid-way through the project or my publicist quit to pursue better opportunities. Patience will help us pray more and keep our sanity during our pursuit of our passion.

FAITH

One of the most important pieces of finding our passions and ourselves is to have the faith to hang in there and see things through and then to have the courage to believe in our faith. I have been in many situations where my faith was tested, hidden, disguised and I was in between a rock and a hard place, but somehow, some way after I stopped worrying and started praying, things started happening because I believed in better days. I do not know how or when the change was going to come, but I kept the faith that it would come. I managed to muster up enough strength and courage to keep my faith up on my worst days, just enough to hold me up until my next good day.

Having faith in a greater good has carried me from the pits to the cloud in the blink of an eye. I could have just quit and given up on life but something instilled in me by my parents and siblings sticks to my soul to believe when there is no reason to believe. My faith has never led me in the wrong direction and has always helped me feel encouraged and stimulated.

We should monitor the things and people we have trust and faith in; we have to have 100% faith in our passion. Our faith will be tested throughout the process of pursuing our passion. "What does faith have to do with passion?" It has everything to do with it. On our journey to find passion followed by purpose, faith will give us comfort along the lonely road of self-discovery. Though we will never be alone, there will be times we need to dig deep inside of us and discover who we really are and what we believe in. Faith will give us the strength to believe in things we cannot see, which is needed when pursuing something we cannot physically touch or see.

Once we begin to develop and believe in our faith nothing can stop us from reaching our goals. My faith has connected me to others, taking me across the world, and given me the confidence to put my ideas on paper. In the end, we must have faith to ascertain our passion, if we do not have the courage to do it, it will never happen.

SELF-LOVE

Before we begin to explore external love for our passion we need to develop love for ourselves. Life is full of mistakes and not loving ourselves is one of the biggest mistakes we could ever make.

I remember when I was younger and into the club scene in Washington D.C. I would treat the nightlife like a fashion show; I had to have the newest kicks and apparel to let the world know I was somebody. In addition, I would purposefully hate on someone who was dressed as good as or better than me. Hating a complete stranger prevented me from loving myself.

The fear of competition was a weakness for me and my competition was perceived as a potential threat, until I started to love myself inside instead of the picture on the outside.

Think of our body as a home, we can design the landscape to appeal to any eye but we have to sleep in the inside of the home. It does not matter how good the house looks on the outside, if the inside is a mess. Think if we approach a house with a terrible yard, I mean toys everywhere, the grass looks like a baseball field and the weeds are all over the house. But then we enter the inside of the house and it is one of the best houses we have seen in our lifetime. We forget about the outside features because the inside is the most important piece to the house. In the home we have love, companionship, security, teamwork, ethics, discipline, motivation, leadership, self-esteem security and many more intangibles. This is also true for our external features, which will bring others into our lives but will not keep them there.

There has to be something beautiful inside us to retain the love and attention of others. We too often fall in love with our external appearance and forget about the beautiful person we have to cultivate inside of us to build up our self-worth and self-esteem. In a world where we will be rejected and not approved by others, it will take a mixture of external love, self-love and knowing our self-worth to get through. We are the only person who knows how to love us the right way.

People come in our lives and try to figure us out, but their guessing and trying to make a guess based on the information we provide to them. Today is a great day to start doing things that make us happy, smile, and bring joy. Often we look for others to satisfy our needs for love, only to realize we own the house with all the love we will ever need.

FOCUS

Growing up in Prince George's County, Maryland we get to see a lot of good basketball all year round, basketball is everywhere. I remember this young kid who would come see us play basketball; he had to be six years old. He would practice our moves and he would do 25 push-ups when his older brother asked him to drop down and give him twenty push-ups. Overall, he was a typical kid and then he started to grow and what made this kid different was his sacrifice and focus.

When he was in junior high, he practiced more than he played around as normal kids did. His grades where already stellar but he stayed in the gym to fine-tune his game and to get better. He was focused on a goal, it was college and he was passionate about it. In high school he was recruited by several major collegiate schools and was rated as one of top point guards in the nations. He was a student of the game, and of life. Most kids in the 10th grade are preoccupied with distractions (sex, dating, clothes, and being crazy), not this kid, something sparked his interest in his passion and he was hungry for more. For example, instead of getting into mischievous activities like most boys his age, he chose to go to the gym. He demonstrated a great deal of focus and maturity as a 10th grader.

Now he is the leader, the soul and the catalyst of the 2014 Georgetown Hoyas and has placed his name among the most talented point guards in the nation. Passion mixed with intensity and consistency is a great remedy for success. Even now as his name is mentioned in the NBA draft Mr. Markel Starks has told reporters he wants to be a Senator one day. I believe he will do it, because once passionate people set their eyes on a goal, they rarely give up on it and are often successful.

Success comes with a price, and the price is called sacrifice and focus. Sacrifice is an intangible skill that all successful leaders have. They all gave up so much of their time, energy and mind for the better good of humanity, which subliminally led them to their purpose. On our journey to success we may sacrifice friendships, leisure activities and social events.

To lead with passion we need to sacrifice things our peers and colleagues may be doing. Passion is not about doing what's hip to others; it's about doing what makes us feel hip to ourselves. I am not surprised by the maturity of Markel; he showed this maturity when he was 6 years old. When a kid works harder than average adults, this is a great sign of a kid with great work ethic and focus.

"Passion cannot be forced upon kids, they need to grow and develop their passion, with continued practice and learning from failure and success."
-Oumar Hill

If it's meant to be, it shall and desire will reveal itself through our intentions. The funny thing about passion is that it permeates through our pores without explanation, but sometimes it is often questioned, "How did he do that? What a great speaker? People can recognize passion and purpose in others from a mile away, the goal is learning how to discover the passion within us first.

HAVE INTANGIBLE SKILLS
"Good character is a priceless possession. Never give it a price tag."
–Linda Hill

I know I am not the most articulate or the best-looking man in the world but I do have valuable characteristics, which separate me from them. I am a people's person, outgoing, great speaker and not afraid of a challenge. These qualities have increased my overall skills-sets tremendously over the years and I have common sense. It takes more than talent to reach the top, the world is full of talented people, but what sets them apart from each other? It's their intangible skills (Listening, pro-activeness, positivity, motivation, dedication and decision making). These key skills have helped keep me in the board meeting so others could get a chance to see my skill sets.

I tell people all the time, "Don't get caught behind your credentials, you may fall short of your potential". We need to work on developing the skills that colleges do not teach. I think sometimes, we tend to hide behind the credentials instead of putting our concepts and ideas on the table to be judged. Talent is important, but talent will not always get us in the house. If we don't want to get kicked out of the house, then we need to develop our intangible skills and continue to grow and learn.

I remember a kid being recruited at our local basketball summer league (www.suburbancoalition.com) and an overseas scout came to check out if he could play. The scout was excited to see the kid, as the kid was excited to see a scout interested in him. The kid was having a great game to me and seemed to hold his own against the current NBA players and did well facing his competition on the court. But the scouts face spoke a different story; he was indifferent to say the least and seemed perplexed. I asked him, "What do you think?" He responded "He is very talented but lacks passion" Then he said, "If he plays at 50% intensity level for free, imagine how you will play when he gets millions. He may not show up for practice. We look for kids with talent and who possess the "it factor". I say all this to say, the agent saw the kid as an investment. His talent served as his credentials but he needed intangible work ethic and his passion for the game to show on the court to give him the opportunity to play overseas.

Think of the life of a rapper. We will look at two rappers, rapper A and B; rapper A is passionate about becoming a rapper, stays up all night practicing his craft, listening to old music and loves the ability to motivate people with his words. On the other hand rapper B is naturally talented with the ability to free style at the drop of a hat; he loves the nice cars and respect. Rapper A will find a way to make it to the studio and find time for developing his craft while Rapper B maybe preoccupied with just the image associated with rapping. Both are talented, but one will be a one hit wonder and another will be around for a decade or longer. Passion will take us places talent cannot go. There has to be a mixture of talent and passion in all things we do.

SELF-EDUCATION

As we begin to ascertain knowledge, we need to marry this knowledge with the wealth of information we already have through self-education, our parents and friends. The lessons we learn along the way are priceless an integral piece to developing ourselves to our fullest potential.

There are many levels to life and maturity, self-education mixed with traditional education will give us an advantage over the typical citizens because we went above and beyond the call of duty to learn something new or existing. Things like this separate the good from the great. These are intangible skills performed in the dark but will shine in the light, once we are called to step up and perform.

For me self-education was greater than my traditional education because it gave me an opportunity to see my full potential to learn and demonstrate what I have learned without any limits. My favorite three ways to learn from self-education is by reading, traveling and loving. I have learned tons of life lessons from each one, come good and bad, but all played a critical part in my development and maturity process. For example, I traveled to Africa to learn more about the country and the culture. In addition, I had a gut feeling about the trip and my friends from Africa who all smiled when I showed interest in their culture and community intrigued me.

Often we get a taste of success and tend to lift our heads up and look down on others, but not me. I treat all people the same, regardless of my success or failure. I have learned through my parents' teaching and my own self-education that karma is real and we should treat others how we want to be treated no matter their financial situation. When we educate ourselves, the information learned prepares us for change, challenges, and adversity.

10 TUMORS, NO EXCUSES

The worst thing we could do with our success is to keep it to ourselves when the world is dying for some type of motivation and inspiration. It gives me great fulfillment to write a book and then hear others can relate to my testimony. I think of myself as a people builder, I specialize in rebuilding people's spirit and energy to keep going.

Passion can spread like a wild fire. I lost my aunt and grandmother to cancer, but somehow I took something from them and it sparked my passion to LiOL (Live Out Loud). I have a friend who lives out loud every day of her life. Meet Teri Holmes. Teri managed to fight and win her battle against brain tumors and now leads a national fight against her battle to help others. Share what you are passionate about with others and you will be satisfied by the reward.

Teri Holmes was a powerful basketball player at Howard University leading the way for her team game after game. Little did she know a decade after college she would be in a game of life or death as she battled tumors in her brain.

Mrs. Holmes, who learned how to write computer code at five years old, won two state basketball championships in high school, took her college team to the NCAA tournament, and maintained a 3.0 GPA. At the tender age of twenty-seven years old, Ms. Holmes was diagnosed with ten brain tumors. I remember in college she was always a little bit different and stood out amongst the other ladies on campus. She had something special about her, she rarely complained and she made a way when there seemed to be no way.

Ms. Holmes underwent a medical procedure called a craniotomy. Craniotomy is a surgical operation in which a bone flap is temporarily removed from the skull to access the brain. Her surgery was successful and Ms. Holmes began her recovery. She maintained the same energy and positive attitude she demonstrated at Howard University. During her recovery she moved from Alexandria, VA back to the west coast to be in the company of her loving mother who helped her focus on recovery and nothing else.

During the hardest times in life, we will discover who our real friends are. When we call a friend, their answers will be direct and solution driven. "What do you need?" "When?" "I am here, so just let me know if you need me". These passion angels are key when we have been knocked down by life and looking for a way to get up.

Ms. Holmes recovered like the champion she has always been. After recovering from her surgery, Ms. Holmes began writing her book titled, *"I survived brain surgery, what's your excuse?"* which is a most have when she releases it! She is also a social media strategist, business owner (TLH Global Vista), marketing director for the Los Angeles Chapter of National Sales Network and even obtained her license to be a spiritual practitioner.

Ms. Holmes faced a life threatening situation head and heart first; she personifies the art of being a passionpreneur, she took an event that could have knocked her out completely and used it to turn her life into a testimony for others to emulate if they encountered similar setbacks. She even took a selfie of her progress from being bald to having a hair full of hair, letting her courage, strength and self-love transfer from her story to others in the world who are facing the same situation and looking for a little motivation. In her picture she held up a sign stating, "I survived brain surgery what's your excuse", just a powerful message full of passion, purpose and favor.

Passion is not about money, it's about a purpose in life to live life the best way we know how and to share our testimonies with others so they do not quit, give up or give into the trials and tribulations of life. Ms. Holmes' entire story gave me goose bumps. She has now joined the National Brain Tumor society and has already participated in an L.A. Brain Tumor walk. In addition, she is raising funds to help eradicate a condition that affects more than 210,000 people in the United States.

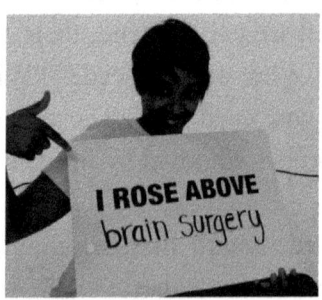

Ms. Holmes stated, these key things helped her get through her ordeal with brain surgery:
1. Stay positive and uplifted in spirit
2. When you have no choice, there is will and faith
3. We will encounter negative events in life, but you have to keep moving.
4. We have to understand we are not our circumstances

5. We are walking testimonies.
6. Personal motto "Shine my light for the world to see. I have this walk that is unique to me. No one else has lived it and no one else can deliver it like I can."

BE YOURSELF
"Passion is not meant to be duplicated but rather originated."
-Oumar Hill

When we meet a person with passion and working in their passion there is something special about that person, they are glowing and breed positivity. We then want to share the feeling we received from this person with others. When growing up searching for a career and profession, it is easy to mimic only what we see, but I had to dig deeper and through self-education found different careers to spark my interest. The first time we see or meet a successful person well dressed, we want to do what they are doing, not knowing what other activities this individual has undertaken to live a high profile life style.

We always assume we can do things others do and better, but we forget to measure the passion and consistency it takes to be successful. When I say be original I do not only mean in actions, but in thought as well. Think with originality and do not conform to what is cool, convenient or acceptable to others. There is no box to confine you! If we try to falsely represent something we are not, we will eventually be revealed and casted out.

I met a young man who said he was dealing with being a virgin at twenty-five years of age and was having some trouble resisting temptation. I first told him I wish I was as brave as him and being a virgin is something, which he should be honored and admired. A virgin is a sign of originality, self-discipline and maturity. Stand up for the purpose of life and live courageously with faith and favor.

Our parents set the foundation. They had the privilege to write the first chapter of our book, but we must finish it with the same tenacity they started it with. We will have several external factors, which will play a major role in our lives. They include mentors, friends, organizations, churches, and educational facilities. Parents have the duty to lay the foundation but we determine our final resting point. We have to stop blaming our parent, because I have seen people in third world countries, where opportunity is far and few between find a way to make a way.

Do not spend too much time complaining and playing the victim, get up, stand up and reach up to victory. It is okay to be different; you have the right to be the best person God has intended you to be. Originality is not only for us, but also for our children as we leave them a footprint in the cement for them to follow and use as a baseline for their life, if necessary. Being original to me is giving the world a piece of our heart, mind and soul, which cannot be replicated. The original people in my life have always had a place in my heart; I respect their opinion and honesty.

PRO BONO

I remember when I first started my journey as a motivational speaker, I was seventeen years old and I would harass my friends who smoked marijuana, "You are going to die!" I was not successful, but I kept trying different things, sometimes knocking the object out of their mouth while they smoked, definitely provoking an altercation of some type.

I was risking my life to save others for free at an early age. This same ritual would follow me my entire life and I still give free information or services away to those in need. I guess I learned it from my mother, who worked in nursing for thirty years. But she did more than nurse patients back to good health, she built relationships and self-esteem in her patients, reassuring everything would be okay and they were in good hands. She would always tell me, "Treat people well, you never know one day you might need them." She loved helping people and she taught me to do the same. Passion is often doing what others will not, no matter how simplistic the task may be.

My dad was the same way, a radiologist by day, but at night he coached basketball and football. He was not paid for his time spent for creating productive men. However, he had the opportunity to see these young men grow up into productive adults. His credibility in the Washington DC area is similar to the Mayor of DC. When I was younger I remember my dad being recruited for a coaching positions for money, but he turned them down. It was not about the money, it was more about the kids.

It is not about the money; sometimes it's about doing a good deed. I created a non-profit for underprivileged youth in the Washington DC metropolitan area called Team Finesse. There was something in me, which moved me to do more in my community. We need to infect the world with love and compassion, less criticism and drama. If we could block out the stress and live wholeheartedly and run towards our dream no matter what obstacles in our way.

We must never stop living and dreaming; if we do, we are technically brain dead. We have this attitude in our late 30s or early 40s of if it hasn't happened by now it will never happen and this is not true. Passion does not care if we win or lose; it's all about the thought, the drive, the sacrifice and the determination to complete what you desire to do. I love people who love what they do; they seem to be more positive and uplifting compared to those that hate what they do and it's understandable.

Message from this chapter: *In the end your destiny is determined by what you have inside of you, what you put into you and providence from God. Take care of your part of the bargain and everything else will take care of itself.*

-SECTION III: BE UNIQUE-

There is only one version of you, will you have the courage to be it, every day?

Chapter 5: PASSIONPRENUERS

"Having the courage to try a new thing is far more important than having the ability to succeed at it"
-Oumar Hill

WHAT IS A PASSIONPRENUER?

Growing up in Maryland in the early nineties I was full of dreams and ambition ready to rule the world. Becoming an entrepreneur was the way for me and the goal was to graduate and make money for myself. I was primarily focused on being financially happy and not following my passion. I graduated, worked hard and I purchased two houses and over the years multiple cars, but something was missing. I continued asking myself, is this it? It could not be. Then I slowly began to reduce my spending and live more frugally. I thought to myself, what would I do without the money? What could I do when I was in my elder years?

This self-analysis produced the word passionpreneur, which is an individual seeking entrepreneurial activities but with the intentions of fulfillment and a better good. Not thinking of financial reward as the primary driver. After the dot.com businesses went under, Wall Street collapse and other down falls of the economies in the world, students have become more focused on living a life of fulfillment and passion, instead of financial reward. (Coleman, Gukati, & Segovia) "It's an era that cries out for new leadership and thinking. And it's an era that has left a generation of young leaders wondering how they can contribute even as they seek a life of meaning, passion and purpose in the private sector.

Whether in the world's biggest corporations, local small and medium business, or nimble start-ups, they aren't entering business solely for financial gain, but as a way to find meaningful work and make a positive difference in the world." A passionpreneur is a designer of their own destiny following their dreams with passion.

In our younger days passionpreneurs maybe be seen as hypertensive or not fitting in the typical learning environment and labeled as having Attention deficit hyperactivity disorder (ADHD) but they are merely looking for different ways to express themselves.

We need to teach our children not only about traditional forms of education but also passionpreneurship opportunities. We need to teach them about how to save money, invest in various markets, and on self-education if college is not an option for them. We need to support our younger generation and help them lead a life of success through following their dream and passion.

Passionpreneurs are individuals who seek out happiness instead of wealth, still in search of freedom and opportunity but for a greater good, business ventures that not only satisfy a financial need but also help them reach the level of self-actualization. These individuals are led by fulfillment and not by financial gain, even though financial wellness will overflow with passion.
-Oumar Hill

There are days where I feel like Rocky Balboa going against the Russian fighter after he beat Apollo. The odds are against me and I have no chance to win and I am getting beat pretty bad by society and my peers, but my passion and faith tells me to keep going.

My passion to educate, lead and motivate others started when I was a little boy and I continued as an adult. When the world knocks us down we have to learn how to jump up with more strength, passion, and purpose. It is the setback, which will set us up for success

SETBACKS=SETUPS AND STEPS UP

In this section we will review some awesome stories of successful passion pioneers who have accomplished a plethora of success. Think of the story regarding the owner of the texting app *"What's App"*, Jan Koum who co-created an independent app, which made him a billionaire when Facebook purchased the app for nineteen billion dollars.

Mr. Koum is a Ukrainian immigrant, who at one point lived on welfare, barely graduated high school and dropped out of college. In addition, both Facebook and Twitter rejected him for a job but he did not let this rejection stop him. Serving as a prime example of never giving up and pushing pass adversity.

Passionpreneurs BELIEVE in their dreams no matter the rejection or setback, as they continually collect resources and information waiting for the right opportunity to show the world their passion. I believe everything happens for a reason and with faith, hard work, continuous practicing we will be ready to not only step up, but step into our passion with purpose.

"Just because you are rejected, non-accepted or considered weird, do not give up on your passion, because your passion will not give up on you"
-Oumar Hill

SUPERSTARS NEVER QUIT

Not all of the rich and famous in the world had an easy road; hence the Huffington Post Article (Jacques, Renee) that details the adversity and rejections some of the most successful people in the world had to endure. These stories will help us understand the sacrifice and determination they exercised to reach success. Some are weird, different, disciplined and dedicated while others are risk takers and courageous, ready to challenge the status quo and reset the standards bar. Let the fun begin.

1. **Failure to owning Microsoft - Bill Gates-** who would have imagined one of the most popular computer designers in the world, would fail at his first attempt at building a computer? That's correct; Bill Gates did with his first attempt at business. Mr. Gate's first business venture, Traf-O-Data (a device which could read traffic tapes) went under.

    It failed so badly, it did not work when Mr. Gates and his partner tried to sell it. But it was the failures from this project, which helped him, launch Microsoft, the world's largest computer software company, which has changed the way we do business. If Bill Gates would have folded up during adversity and gave up, we may have never had the creation of Microsoft. His success has continued on to his creation of the Bill and Melinda Gates foundation, which has become the world's largest philanthropy organization helping people all over the world.

2. **Called crazy as a child to becoming a genius, Albert Einstein-**He was one of the greatest thinkers of all time. He did not talk until he was four, was considered lazy and unproductive by his teachers in elementary school, and he often created abstract questions people couldn't comprehend. However, he never stopped thinking and challenging his own mind, eventually created the theory of relativity and remains in our history books for his innovation and creativity.

    In 1921 Mr. Einstein won the Nobel Peace Prize for his theory, which would contribute to the development of several innovations such as the television, remote control devices, automatic door openers, lasers, and DVD-players. Passionate people have a way of being weird, unconventional and confusing to some, but never second-guess your passion.

3. **Homeless to superstardom, Jim Carrey-** He is a well-known actor all over the world who was once homeless living with his family in a van. In addition, Mr. Carrey had to drop out of school to support his family. Now he is one of the funniest, well-known comedians in the world. Who would have thought this? I would have never imagined this after first seeing Mr. Carrey on TV starring on the show In Living Color.

    The passion Mr. Carrey displays during his performances are smile and laughter worthy and he gives every inch of his soul to his audience. Maybe it was the adversity, which fuels his passion to be successful and remain there. There is always an opportunity to generate a positive outcome out of a negative situation, but it is solely the responsibility of the participants. Mr. Carrey decided to chase his dreams and never look back to being homeless.

4. **Surfing above all odds, Bethany Hamilton-**I remember hearing about a young surfer who was one of the best teenage surfers if not the best at the age of 12 years old. Meet Bethany Hamilton who had the world in her hand at 13years old and successful in her craft of surfing and taking the world by storm with her smile and charm. Only to have her arm taken off a year later from a shark attack. But she did not quit or fold, instead she became bold and a month later she was back in the water surfing again.

    A shark has never bitten me and I am a bit nervous swimming in water, so I can imagine the psychological dilemma she was facing when she decided to go back in the water and do what she loved. She not only got back on the board, but she continued to compete at a high level, reaching 5th on her next tournament since the attack but eventually winning 1st in her next five major tournaments. Not to mention writing two books about her ordeal and a movie. Her determination to make the most out of life is to be honored and shared with the world. She is a passionpreneur for life!

5. **Dyslexia to having his own island, Sir Richard Charles Nicholas**-The greatest accomplishment in the world is to have a weakness and turn that weakness into strength. This successful person suffered dyslexia and grew up to be the owner of his own island. His headmaster told Mr. Branson at the age of 15 years old he was going to be in prison or a millionaire. His head master was wrong; he became a billionaire and the 6th richest person in London according to Forbes magazine.

    How does a boy with dyslexia manage to leave school, start a magazine, and then a record company and eventually own over 400 companies? The character and spirit of Mr. Branson is similar to James Bond in 007 movies, using his charm and charisma to save the world and handle his business.

6. **Rejection to 350 million sold, Stephen King**-Growing up I watched all of his scary horror movies but I did not know this legend had a rough start with his first novel being turned down thirty times by publishing houses. Mr. King has sold over three hundred and fifty million copies of his books, most of them turned into feature films, television shows and comic books. According to Huffington Post, if it

was not for his wife Carrie, Stephen King may have never existed.

After being rejected by numerous publishing companies, Mr. King threw his manuscript in the trash, only to have his wife come behind him and retrieve the document and urged her husband to keep going, don't quit. Since that encouragement he has delighted the world with numerous best sellers in movies and books. His wife saw something in him that he did not see in himself amidst the rejection and disappointment but in the end he trusted his wife and stuck with his passion. He has been entertaining the world ever since, thanks to his wife.

7. **Poor to owning her own network, Oprah Winfrey**-One of the most influential, and powerful women in America is Oprah Winfrey, but her road to success was not an easy one, especially as a child. Oprah was repeatedly molested by her cousin, uncle and family friend as a child and eventually would run away from home. She then at the age of fourteen gave birth to a baby boy who died shortly after. Oprah did not let this horrible beginning deter her from a beautiful ending. Oprah was so poor she would steal money from her mother to keep up with her peers. Even when she tried to report the abuse to her family members at the age of twenty-four years old, they did not believe her.

Going back and forth from her mother's house in Wisconsin to her dad's house in Nashville, Tennessee Ms. Winfrey focused on her education and the rest is history. From rags to riches she went from movies, to owning her own television show, to owning her own television channel Oprah Winfrey Network. She never gave up, even when others did not believe in her. She never blamed anyone for their bad decisions; she took her knocks in life and keeps on getting up. Over the years she has created various philanthropy programs, school, and initiatives to help underserved youth in the United States and other continents.

Some of us get knocked down and stay down blaming everybody in our peripheral vision, while others like Ms. Winfrey get knocked down and find a way to always get up, over and through any situation. There is strength in getting up; this is evident in Oprah Winfrey's continuous leadership and success.

Most people quit after making a quick buck but these successful individuals took success to the next level. When we lead with passion we tend to challenge the standards set before us and set the bar higher than before. The burning desire to be the best is what we all strive for. I could only imagine the additional adversity and pressure they received from obtaining their wealth. Please take note and apply the same principles to your life.

BENEFITS OF FOLLOWING YOUR PASSION

In today's society we are bombarded with negativity, stress and drama. It is like when the weather is sunny one day, but eventually it will rain, and passion will be our umbrella. Passion protects me from getting wet and provides a positive force field in my life, when the days look bleak. Passion turns my weakness into strength and gives me a since of everything will be okay. We are subjected to negativity daily, and we have to become a sponge of positivity to reach and our goals with compassion. A person who can stand up with passion during the face of adversity can stand anything. Standing with passion is living with love.

BENEFITS LIST

1. **Leadership.** Society is full of change, rejection, and bad leadership. The individuals who muster the courage, determination and fortitude to lead with passion often sacrifice the most, such as social life, leisure activities, and relationships. Leaders spend the majority of their time and energy on activities, which bear the most "return on passion investment" (RPaI).

   Most of the leaders in this generation lead with a passion; whether it is for President Obama working toward change, or President Nelson Mandela's quest for equality, something within them drives them to push pass the normalcy of life and lead with passion to go above the call of duty and serve as a role model for billions. These individuals are/were passionpreneurs, and passionpreneurs make it their business to lead with passion.

2. **Community development.** With the building of passionate leaders, we will foster a domino effect of passion and positivity within the community we reside in and pass through. I took a journey to Ethiopia, Africa a few months ago with my best friend, NuNu Wako and my brother from another mother Eagle Mate.

   We passed through twenty different cities in Ethiopia, meeting different ethnicities along the way and learning various cultures. I could visually see the joy both of my friends brought to their families' faces once they returned to their homeland. It was refreshing to say the least, to see two successful kids from Ethiopia raised in the U.S. come back to their native country and provide support for their families. The people just wanted love and they both provided a wealth of love, knowledge and compassion for their culture and values. All of the people there were as curious about me as I was curious about them; it was a passionate friendship made in heaven.

The passion I have for people, humanity, and educating others permeated throughout the people I contacted all throughout Ethiopia. Sometimes being referred to as Gabe, meaning "lost son", God's gift or Gods son, they thought highly of me and I thought higher of them. Passion is habit forming, whether it is good or bad passion.

3. **Fuels success.** If we do not have passion in the things we do, we will function like a time bomb waiting to explode. Instead of counting the hours within the day, we should love every minute of each day wishing there was more time added to the day to do more. A person leading with passion will spend the majority of their time thinking and working hard to figure out the next steps.

Passion fuels success because it gives us the extra fuel to get over the hump. When my supervisor in the government rejected my promotion and said I did not seem fit to receive a promotion, I just smiled and said thank you, because I knew I was worthy of so much more. Eventually her director noticed my work and she was forced to give me a promotion. When we think we have created our last inspiration, passion will give us one more idea.

4. **Builds Confidence.** Passion builds confidence in everything we do. While working for the Department of Education, I was directed to present training on a software program for program managers. This is basically a tool to track funding for projects throughout the life of the project. I was nervous but not afraid of the task. I remember going into the first dry run for the training with my colleagues. As I started reading the slide verbatim, and mid-presentation, I was stopped by one of my colleagues who seemed perplexed. She took me

outside the room and told me I needed to really go practice this presentation and brings my best effort to the table.

Sometimes the only time we can see ourselves is through the eyes of our peers. I realized my presentation was inadequate and so I began to practice and rehearse gaining more and more confidence reducing the usage of slides and using more of the information I had stored inside my head. Her comment brought me down but it also gave me something to strive for. I made my presentation and gained confidence in the training, the system, and myself as the trainer. One apple can spoil a bunch, but one good seed can start a garden of positivity.

5. **Perseverance.** We have all heard of Michael Jordan talking about being cut from his high school basketball team, Nelson Mandela being incarcerated for nine thousand days in prison because of his fight for freedom, or the number of courageous women all across the globe who have defeated breast cancer and are now leading a legacy about persevering and never giving up. There are many stories I could have included in this paragraph but I choose to recognize my mother's again for her continuous passion for herself and her family.

As I stated before, she was treated for a rare illness, which forced her to undergo brain surgery without prior notice. Not to mention her passion to overcome post-surgery and a divorce. My mother had to readjust her life from the bottom in her fifties after being married for thirty years and she did it seamlessly. Somehow she found the courage and strength to make things okay, when they seemed destined for destruction. During her separation, my mother would say, "What other choice do I have but to stand up with love once my love was taken away from me".

My mother still has a very good relationship with my father. He calls to make sure I send flowers on Mother's Day and her birthday and I can see the friendship between the two of them will never change. When we are going through some hard times we need to hold on until the next day and take it one day at a time. Passion will help us heal, see the big picture and overcome our setbacks.

6. **Better love life.** Once we infuse passion within our career it will trickle down within our relationships. It is inevitable that the passion we instill in our work ethic will find a way into our love life. Think about the first question we ask on a date, "What do you do for a living?" and the response, "I work for the police department" versus an answer that shows passion for a career, "I work for a law enforcement agency and my dad was a police officer for ten years. I arrested a model today who looked just like you, she was arrested for being too beautiful".

As a man finds his purpose in life or a career he loves he will be excited to share his journey with others. The passion Jay-Z has for his business, music and friends has led him to the top of the world and now he has Beyoncé, which makes him the king of all kings. I think what makes Jay-Z, Jay-Z is his crazy work ethics and I think if he wasn't rapping, he still would be doing something for not only himself but also his family and friends. Some people are just passionpreneurs, it's not just about them, and it's about passion with purpose.

Finding our passion comes with big reward. Not only does loving what we do make us work harder, but it also makes us think about the work and makes us smarter. When we are passionate about our career we will give everything to make sure we are successful. This work ethic is attractive to the opposite sex and is used as a measuring tool for capability and ambition. Yes, following our passion will bring us love. Passion cannot only bring us great reward, but it could bring us our soul mate.

Message from this chapter: *Your uniqueness is the platform for your success, regardless how weird it maybe or out of the ordinary. You have to believe in your uniqueness and defy the odds.*

CHAPTER 6: REAL LIFE PASSIONPRENUERS

Now we have a better understanding of what a passionpreneur means, let's review some real life passionpreneurs' responses to a brief questionnaire I created to get their opinion on how passion has played a role in their life and what it means to them. These are passionpreneurs I met during my journey around the world and they do not know each other. These are real life people with real life struggles, doubt, and stress, but somehow, some way, they mustered enough energy and determination to get up, keep going and let passion be their guide.

Often times, we lack the strength to get up and we do not believe we have the strength, but if we surround ourselves with success stories of perseverance, we have no choice but to get up. The purpose of this section is to give a glimpse into the mindset of passionpreneurs and an understanding how they think. I also have provided some analysis of what I gained from each interview and the similarities amongst all the interviews. I wanted to share their point of views on what passion is from their perspective. I not only admire these individuals but they all bring different intangible skills to the table and will be future leaders in their respective areas.

"My heroes are those who risk their lives every day to protect, teach and improve our world and make it a better place—teachers, parents, social workers, counselors, police, firefighters, and members of our armed forces."
-Oumar Hill

Nazley Omar
Teacher, World Traveler, Lover of Life
In Vietnam by way of Johannesburg, South Africa

The first passionpreneur is Nazley Omar from Johannesburg, South Africa. She is a journalist, frequent flyer, and teacher of passion. She has been all over the world and had the opportunity to visit some places I only dream of visiting one day, including Thailand, China, Malaysia, and Egypt. She has the cunning ability to create a story through her writing in the South African paper, in which she has taken her passion from the paper to reality to live her dreams in various parts of the world.

Continuously spreading knowledge and love, this passionpreneur has always captured my attention with wit, intellect, and passionate characteristics very few have - courage and determination not to settle for what society has presented to her. She may be short in stature, but she has the passion of thirty men.

1. *What does passion mean to you? What is the same passion you had as a child? What will you teach your child in regards to passion, purpose and Getting up after being knocked down?* Passion is about pursuing what makes your soul smile. It all comes down to doing more

of what makes you feel alive, empowered, inspired and hopeful. I realized from a young age that writing is what I was meant to do and I've pursued my passion relentlessly. I will tell my children that in this world, opportunities abound and the world is theirs for the taking; they just need to have the courage to go for it.

2. *Tell me a story about a turning point (positive or negative) and how you utilized that moment to become the successful person you are today. Describe your feeling before, during, and after this moment.*
   a. After I finished school, I worked hard and managed to land a great job at one of South Africa's most respected magazines. After working there for three years, I became bored and uninspired. I was in an unfulfilling relationship and I just felt completely stuck. I then went to Malaysia on holiday and everything just clicked into place. I knew that South Africa was no longer the place I needed to be. When I returned from my holiday, I began a teaching course, did plenty of research and found a job in South Korea. I moved six months later.
   b. *Describe any passion angels (people who changed your life) that helped you during this time.* My mother offered me her unwavering support.

3. *When you were younger what skills/training/teaching/mentoring helped you?*
Education is key. The only reason I was able to find a well-paying job and move abroad in just a few months was because I had the qualifications to back it up. Also, staying abreast with what's happening in the world is

important. The world extends far beyond your town, state and country.
4. *What would you tell the younger generation following your career path? What tools should they utilize?* Changing your life comes down to identifying what makes you happy and then finding a way to make a living out of it. Do plenty of research and network! All of the jobs I have had since leaving South Africa came about through referrals or word-of-mouth. Work hard; maintain your integrity and you will be rewarded.
5. When you are having a bad day, what techniques or ritual do you utilize to change your day? If not change your day, what do you do to make sure you have a productive day? For example: I pray, read, or call my mom. I believe in shaking it off. A bad day is a bad day but it always draws to an end. Tomorrow is a new start, embrace it!

Nazley's Interview Points:
- Bad days have endings. Tomorrow is a new start; embrace it
- Work hard, maintain integrity, and you will be rewarded

- Passion is about pursuing what makes your soul smile. It all comes down to doing more of what makes you feel alive, empowered, inspired and hopeful.
- Pursue your passion relentlessly and have courage to follow your passion and dreams.
- Education is key and make sure you have the credentials to back your passion up.

Poet, New York, USA
In New York City by way of Haiti

The next passionpreneur is located in the busiest place in the United States of America - New York City, by way of Haiti. She is a poet, songwriter, and YouTube producer of enlightening movements, yoga fanatic, and a really good person. She is an independent business owner and is very passionate about life. She has shared with me delightful poems when I was down and needed some mental stimulation. The following are her answers about passion and what it means to her as she deals with managing relationships and her business.

1. *What does passion mean to you? Was it the same passion you had as a child? What will you teach your child in regards to passion, purpose and getting up after being knocked down?* Passion is that stirring in your soul, that won't let you quit, no matter what. I definitely wasn't. As a child, I was more motivated by pleasing my parents, regardless of if I was passionate about it or not. So I put their needs/wants before mines. Well, first off, I don't want to dictate my wants for my children on them; it is

their life at the end of the day. I want to have conversations with them, to find out what they want and are passionate about, providing it isn't harmful to them. Once we get there, and they know they have my support, I will tell them that during those times, go play, have fun, take your mind off...and let IT come to you.

2. *Tell me a story about a turning point (positive/negative) and how you utilized that moment to become the successful person you are today.* I recently started seeing someone and we started dating. While I was getting to know him, my best friend (we were two peas in a pod), was getting upset that I wasn't spending enough time with her. We were also building a business at the time, so we would go to networking events but not too many events. So about a couple of weeks into me dating him, she and I had an event with another friend.

    Afterwards, we were discussing how it went, and just chatting and that's when everything came to a head. She said I had changed and that I knew that the month was hard for her, but I wasn't available. I acknowledged that we hadn't hung out, but I also needed space to enjoy this, and she had to understand. But she wanted no part of it, said she needed a break and a couple of months later, and sent me a break-up text. It hurt, like hell. It felt like I didn't deserve to be happy, because it hurt her. How could she "break-up" when we were supposed to be friends? Why couldn't we work through this, especially since we were elevating ourselves spiritually? Wasn't this one of the mantras, forgiveness, working through tough times?

    As time went on, I realized that this was my lesson; I put her happiness before mine. I catered to her needs and not to my own. It taught me a valuable lesson - to never do that again, and to put me first. So I have used that to gain my independence from relying and doing things to please others, and pursuing what I want. If I can't please me, then no one else will be able to.

3. *When you were younger what skills/training/teaching/mentoring helped you? What would you tell the younger generation, following your career path? What tools should they utilize?* They need to develop patience, with themselves. But then again, to practice and teach yoga, you should already know that.

4. *When you're having a bad day, what techniques/rituals do you utilize to change your day? If not change your day, what do you do to at least make sure you have a productive day?* This is a tough one, because I sometimes, need to stay in that place for a bit, because it helps me gain clarity. I will usually, want to be alone, maybe watching some movies, or read. But lately, I've been writing poetry, to get my thoughts out.

Haitian's Interview Points:
- When you are going through difficult times, find your place to gain clarity.
- Please yourself first. If I can't please me, then no one else will be able to.
- Gain your mental independence.
- Don't put other people in control of your happiness or passion.
- Passion is that stirring in your soul, that won't let you quit, no matter what.

Paul Hovan Jr,
Transformation Specialist & Fitness Guru,
Connecticut, USA

This guy is intelligent beyond his years. He is a motivational speaker waiting to be called. He is a personal trainer, and, like most personal trainers, he works to bring the most out of his clients, but does it by example and with intense passion. His words build passion with purpose. A passionpreneur will die for what they believe in because they are 125% devoted to their craft and making it become successful. If we can transform our body from the size of a sumo wrestler to the size of a super model, we are pretty passionate about our health and well-being. This is the most passionate personal trainer I know!

1. *What does passion mean to you? Was it the same passion you had as a child? What will you teach your child in regards to passion, purpose and getting up after being knocked down?* To me, passion is all about having a burning desire to do something. If I can describe it in my own way, I would say that if you truly had a passion for something, it should feel like your soul is literally on fire

for that particular thing. It is something that wakes you up every day.

It is something that you can't help but smile when thinking about. It is what gives your life a purpose. It is what helps you continue along your journey after many, many obstacles have already presented themselves in your path. To achieve a certain goal or dream you have, it takes an immense amount of time and energy. If you don't have a passion for that goal or dream, you will give up on it because along the road toward your goals, there will be many challenges and tough situations that present themselves to you.

Why try so hard, put so much effort and time into achieving something that you don't even really care if you didn't achieve? Exactly. You wouldn't. No sane person would either. But if you have a passion for the goal, a love for it, a burning desire in your soul for it, you will certainly not give up, no matter how tough and challenging it gets.
Giving up just isn't an option. In my head, once I set a goal I have a passion to achieve it. It's not a matter of "if" I will achieve that goal, only a matter of "when". I'm willing to die for the things I want to achieve. That may be too extreme for some, but it is not for me, and I believe that is why I have experienced the amount of success I have thus far at the young age of 22. You have to be willing to die for what you believe in. If you are not, then it does not mean that much to you.

I will teach my child/children the same lessons my parents have taught me. If you work hard, and never give up, you can become anything you want to become. They never doubted me, and I will never doubt my child/children either. They never told me that I couldn't achieve every goal that I told them about, and I will never tell my child/children they can't achieve their goals either. Through my darkest and most dreadful times, they never gave up on me, and I will never give up on my child/children.

2. *Tell me a story about what changed/enhanced/turning point (positive or negative) and how you utilized that moment to become the successful person you are today.* Despite being overweight in high school, I suffered a very painful injury my freshman year of college when I was 18 years old. This was after my first two Natural Bodybuilding competitions and shortly after my first photo shoot. I was on a high, looking and feeling great. After placing well in my first two-bodybuilding shows and then doing my first photo shoot ever, I was on top of the world, so to speak.

About a month later, I woke up one morning in December and couldn't even lift my left arm. It was odd because the night before, I was perfectly fine (or so I thought). I trained chest and triceps and did 45 minutes of cardio. I can remember it like it was yesterday. I immediately knew something was wrong, but my first thought going through my head was, "I'm never going to be able to lift or compete ever again." I ended up having a cyst lying dormant on the nerves of my trapezius muscle and deltoid. I ended up doing 6 months of physical therapy, which I was told would shrink the cyst and possibly make it disappear and that I'd be back to training very shortly, but that wasn't the case. I needed to have surgery to remove the cyst and also have certain nerve tunnels cleared that were filled with scar tissue and damaged cells.

I remember going into my first physical therapy session, and my first "exercise" was to lean on a table and move my arm in a circular motion. Needless to say, I fell into a depression and couldn't get the thoughts out of my head that I would never be back to what I once was.

However, I did not give up, and I did not give any more energy into those negative thoughts. I continued going to physical therapy three times each week. I did additional exercises when I got home. I approached every session with my physical therapist as I would a session in the gym - with intensity, a positive mind-set, and a chance for myself to improve. It took me two and a half long years, but here I am... back, bigger, and better than ever. It's those types of experiences in your life that develop your strength, faith, and a new type of mental fortitude that other situations just would not enable you to do.

I always tell people, don't look down on the experiences of your past good and bad, they have all developed you into the person you are today. You are a better person because of the things you have been through, and you couldn't have become the person you are today any other way.

3. *When you were younger what skills/training/ teaching/mentoring helped you?* To be honest, I never had any type of [professional] training or mentoring when I was younger. My parents have been teaching me and mentoring me since the day I was born. I'd say that they've done a pretty good job.

4. *What would you tell the younger generation following your career path? What tools should they utilize?* I would tell them that patience is a very real thing. In the beginning, I wanted everything NOW. I would put so much pressure on myself to get things done that I would lose sight of some of the things that really mattered most (family, balance, rest, prayer).

There is absolutely no substitute for hard, focused work. It seems that now a days, people want a quick fix with everything. If they want to make more money, they try and figure out the easiest way to do it. If they want to lose weight and become fit, they look for the easiest way to get it done. No one wants to work hard anymore. No one wants to devote his or her time toward work. They want to go out, have fun, party, and then at their job, they do the exact minimum just to get by.

People settle too quickly now days. I would also tell them that dreams are a very real thing. Once you have a dream or thought in your head, and then you say it with words or write it down on paper, it becomes real. Dreams can come true, but you have to be willing to pay the price and make sacrifices if you want to see them become your reality. It doesn't matter what other people have to say about the things you want to accomplish. It's not their journey; they are not supposed to understand why you do what you do. If no one else believes in you, it doesn't matter.

As long as you believe in yourself, anything is possible.

5. *When you are having a bad day what techniques or ritual do you utilize to change your day? If not change your day, what do you do to make sure you have a productive day? For example: I pray, read, or call my mom.* If I'm having a bad day, I try and think about the people who have it much worse than me. Too often we get caught up in our lives and think we have it so bad. We drop our coffee and all of the sudden the rest of our day is horrible. We hit some traffic on our way to work and now we're unhappy for the rest of the day.

Meanwhile, there are people in other countries without running water, without a roof over their heads, without shoes to walk in, without clothes to wear. This way of thinking that I have developed did not happen overnight. I have been through many tough times in my life, but I always knew that God wanted it that way. We try and figure out everything in our life, but forget that God is directing our steps every day.

There is a reason things happen to you and only you. As time passes, God will make these things clearer to you. I read verses from the Bible every day. God's word is powerful and has helped me develop the strength, faith, work ethic, attitude, love, and passion I feel toward others at this very moment. Never forget, God turns setbacks into set ups, stormy nights into beautiful sunrises, and can turn the weakest coward into the strongest warrior.

Hov's Interview Points:
- Passion is not a matter of "if" I will achieve that goal, only a matter of "when".
- Passion can defeat anything, including obesity and depression.
- God is directing our steps every day. There is a reason things happen to you, and only you. As time passes, God will make these things clearer to you.
- Read verses from the Bible every day. God's Word is powerful and will help you develop the strength, faith, work ethic, attitude, love, and passion.

Dr. Maurice Lee
Pharmacist, Author & Philanthropist,
South Carolina, USA

This passionpreneur is a jack of all trades, coming from a small town in North Carolina to becoming bigger than life, by not listening to his doubters and continuing to believe in hard work and having the guts to put his life on the line. His accomplishments include making it out of his small town, becoming a well-respected pharmacist, recognized author, actor, philanthropist, singer and motivational speaker. This passionpreneur is awesome. When life handed him lemons he made lemonade and then turned it into Gatorade. He took the cards life dealt him, made the best with those cards and made the lives of others better. Some people will stop at success, but others will push past success to open the door for other to come through. The abbreviation Dr. does not serve him justice for the opportunities he has brought to the community in North Carolina.

1. *What does passion mean to you?* Passion to me is the act of expressing a strong emotion to a particular desire or goal.
2. *Is it the same passion you had as a child?* As a child, I was very ambitious, always wanting to pursue various career

options. As an adult, I find myself still possessing the same passion for ambition as I am always finding ways to expand my resume. There's a quote that's states "In order for a man to be great, his reach must always exceed his grasp."

3. *What will you teach your child in regards to passion, purpose and getting up after being knocked down?* I will teach my child the importance of truly understanding what he/she is passionate about and to always be true to their passion. One important rule I will teach is that if you are knocked down 6 times, be sure to get up 7 times

4. *Tell me a story about a turning point (positive or negative) and how you utilized that moment to become the successful person you are today.* I had a summer job during one of my college breaks. One of the older co-workers asked me, "What are you going to college for?" I replied, "To become a doctor." His reply after looking me up and down, "You might make it." While some may view that as negative energy towards me, I utilized that as motivation to excel and doubt the naysayers.

> a. *Describe your feeling before, during, and after this moment.* Before that event, I was very confident in knowing that I would become 'that doctor'. During that event, for a brief moment doubt began to overshadow my lifelong dream of becoming a doctor. After the event, I pulled my thoughts together and prayed to God saying, "Let thy will be done".
>
> b. *Describe any passion angels (people who changed your life) that helped you during this time.* My mother has definitely been my "passion angel" because she taught me to never allow the negative opinion or words from others to detour me from the journey God placed me on to arrive to my destiny.

5. *When you were younger what skills/training/teaching/mentoring helped you?* When I was younger, I adopted the skill of reading. I understood at a very young age the importance of this skill as it increased knowledge on all levels. As I matriculated through my educational career, it was easy for me to develop studying habits due to my hunger for reading.
6. *What would you tell the younger generation following your career path? What tools should these utilize?* I would encourage them to first study the number of careers that are available. Then, choose a "career", not a job that you will be passionate about and enjoy waking up to everyday. Never choose a career based off of the annual salary!
7. *When you are having a bad day what techniques or ritual do you utilize to change your day? If not change your day, what do you do to make sure you have a productive day? For example: I pray, read, or call my mom.* First, I pray. Second, I talk to my mother. Third, I turn on the music of Donny Hathaway or Gladys Knight

Dr. Lee's Survey Points:
- If you are knocked down six times, be sure to get up seven times.
- What some view as negative energy towards me, I utilized that as motivation to excel and doubt the naysayers.
- Doubt can only temporarily prevent you from obtaining your goal, but passion will take you to the Promised Land.
- Education and reading are very power tools and will stay with you for the duration of your life.
- Choose a "career", not a job that you will be passionate about and enjoy waking up to everyday. Never choose a career based off of the annual salary

Kelani Haralson
Entrepreneur,
Chicago, USA

Kelani is first and foremost a child of God. Her faith holds a high place in her life because she knows it's only because of God that she is blessed. She is an introverted entrepreneur who lives to create and is at her happiest when she is handling her business and making the world better. She prefers being in the background, but I persuaded her to include herself in this survey to share her opinion regarding passion.

1. *What does passion mean to you? What it the same passion you had as a child? What will you teach your child in regards to passion, purpose and getting up after being knocked down?*

    My definition of passion is as follows

    Passion- having a strong, burning desire for something personally fulfilling.

    a. No, it doesn't mean the same from when I was a kid. It changed slightly because I now have a better understanding of it.
    b. When I have a child I will teach them to be passionate about God and everything He cares

for because not all things we're passionate about is good. I will teach them in order to find your purpose, get before God and ask Him to reveal it because everyone is born with an assignment from Him. I will also let them know it doesn't make you a failure if you're knocked down. Just get back up, shake it off and proceed.

2. *A story about what changed/enhanced/turning point (positive or negative) and how you utilized that moment to become the successful person you are today.*
    a. In November of 2010 I was laid off my job…my good paying job as a medical coder. I had a mortgage, car, bills and in the mist of all that I called off my engagement. Things were really bad to say the least. After 2 years of not working my unemployment benefits ran out and I had little income (around $400 a month and was taking care of my grandfather. I went on countless job interviews. Some looked promising, but I was told I was overqualified…really?

    I decided to go back to wearing my natural hair for many reasons. I was really into researching how to care for my hair then I started making my own products. Little did I know I was going to start a business making all-natural hair and skin products? I've always known I was supposed to be my own boss but while I was medical coder making good money I got comfortable. Now I say being laid off was the best thing that could of happened to me. My outlook is different.
    b. *Describe your feeling before, during, and after this moment.*
    Before I took the steps to start my business I was

excited because I'm a "big picture" person, but I almost quit before I initially got started (LOL). I was offered to be a vendor at an event.

I like to meet deadlines before the deadline in most cases so for this particular event it was no different. I put in my orders for raw ingredients from my suppliers weeks in advance. They messed up my order so I ended up getting everything a week before the event and did I mention I made the products myself? So while I'm pressing, making products a few days before the event, I broke down crying wanting to throw in the towel. I was overwhelmed and I thought, "What am I doing?"

I called a friend and he encouraged me to stick it out. I did and the event was a success. I am a believer so I pray over my business even before I started. I knew as soon as I went into business "for real" it would take off quickly and knowing that I was hesitant because I was afraid, afraid of failing but that's where my faith in God comes in. He keeps me going.

    a. Passion angels- I have many. I am blessed because people I know who are successful in their own right have given me whatever I needed be it advice, helping hands, etc. But my mother is my number one passion angel because as soon I told her about my business plans she was on board and she invests in my business.

3. *When you were younger, what skills/training /teaching/mentoring helped you?*

My love for research has helped tremendously. In my

business, research is imperative, and of course teaching from the bible works for every area of my life.
4. *What would you tell the younger generation following your career path? What tools should these utilize?* I would tell the younger generation to never stop learning, researching and pursue being the best. Every success is a prayer of success and every failure is because of failing to pray (words I've been taught from my pastor Bishop Keith Butler)
5. *When you are having a bad day what techniques or ritual do you utilize to change your day? If not change your day, what do you do to make sure you have a productive day. For example: I pray, read, or call my mom.* When having a bad day I pray, get in my word and talk to my circle.

Kelani's Survey Point:
- To find purpose submit yourself to God and ask for Guidance.
- Keep a circle of friends we can call on during a time of need.
- Research your passion again and again.
- Never Stop Learning
- Every success is a prayer success and every failure is a failure to pray.

Silas Grant
Community Activist,
Founder of Information Age
Washington DC, USA

The next passionpreneur is nicknamed the street mayor in Washington D.C. because he does so much for the community from which he was raised, ranging from Stop the Violence campaign, to bike riding programs to reduce pollution, to developing a program to serve senior citizens in the community free Turkeys for thanksgiving holiday. In his spare time, he has served on various communities for the District of Columbia Government. He has created a website to inspire and lead the youth called "The Information Age" (www.informationage.co).

1. *What does passion mean to you? What it the same passion you had as a child? What will you teach your child in regards to passion, purpose and getting up after being knocked down?*

There's a saying: "energy goes where attention flows". I believe that passion is directly connected to what you pay attention to. As you grow, you should gain exposure to different ideas, concepts and experiences. For me, I believe that my passion is somewhat the same as it was when I was a child. However, my experiences have broadened my horizons and given me a clearer perspective on what I should be spending my time doing. If I had a child, I'd teach him/her in order to operate within your passion; you have to be prepared to defend your cause. Defending an argument is the most important skill that a younger person can have in their arsenal. Defending an argument involves knowing the facts and the truth. Passion can be dangerous when we disregard the facts and the truth. The facts and the truth should govern our passion. When we fall down, we can analyze our setbacks or lack of progress against the facts and the truth.

2. Share *a story about what changed/enhanced/turning point (positive or negative) and how you utilized that moment to become the successful person you are today. a. Describe your feeling before, during, and after this moment. b. Describe any passion angels (people who changed your life that helped you during this time.*

A turning point in my life was the beginning of my relationship with the woman who is now my wife. I met my wife when I was 26. Most of my friends and associates were working toward success. However, I can't say that most of us were really determined to follow a set plan. Our passion for our respective plans seemed to be all over the place. When I met my wife, she was the first person that I'd met in my age bracket that was absolutely determined to live out her life the way that she'd plan to. Her presence in my life was a motivating factor for my own life plan. Before I met her, I was unsure of what to do. In those early moments in our friendship, her presence was refreshing. Since those early moments, I've been able to see my life plan even clearer. I'd never heard of the term "passion angel" until now. I'd certain nominate my wife as a passion angel of mine.

3. When you were younger what skills/training/ teaching/mentoring helped you?

As a child, I was taught to be patient, respectful and considerate. Those are not just attributes. Having patience, respect, and consideration for others is a skill that can be developed. Because my goals are largely in the area of social entrepreneurialism and public service, I have to work with people and understand their needs to get my goals accomplished. Without a doubt, patience, respect and consideration for others are skills that are necessary to be successful in these arenas.

4. What would you tell the younger generation following your career path? What tools should these utilize?

For young people entering the fields of social entrepreneurialism and public service, understand that both fields are evolving. The impact of social media can be an asset or a liability to your success. Your public and private lives are both on display for the world to see. The trust that people have for you and the ability for them to rely on you will be pertinent to your success. I would suggest that exercising your ability to increase your patience, respect, and consideration levels for other people is extremely important.

5. When you are having a bad day, what techniques or ritual do you utilize to change your day? If not change your day, what do you do to make sure you have a productive day. For example: I pray, read, or call my mom.

Bad days come along when you're attempting to live within your passion. I read an article recently about procrastination. The author suggested that we all have procrastination meters within. Whenever we have a task and we begin thinking of other things to do, that's when our meter should go off. The task that we are avoiding is ultimately the task that will get us closer to our goal. Sometimes the task is so large that we lose our spirit and our day becomes a bad one. The best technique for bad days is reclaiming control of every day. You can't control every encounter and activity. However, for all the things that you can control, by all means, take control. Assess your bad days and figure out what were the events in that day that you could've taken control of. When you see a bad day approaching, stop and assess what you can do to regain control of the day. Along those lines, a personal tip that I use is my anticipation of an event or activity that will happen after a difficult day. If I know that Monday will be a day filled with encounters that I have no desire to deal with, I'll think about a fun activity that I'm anticipating that takes place later that evening or the next day. When I complete the task that I didn't want to endure, I have a fun activity waiting after that is over. Also, prayer is important. I don't pray to change the circumstances. My prayers generally involve me asking God to remind of all the things that I've been taught about his work and all that I've learned naturally will be brought back to my remembrance.

Silas's Survey Points:
- Passion can be dangerous when we disregard the facts and the truth.

- Increase the skills of practicing patience, respect, and consideration for others.
- Reclaim control of every day by taking control of the things you can control.
- Do not pray to change the circumstances, but instead pray for a reminder of all the lessons learned.
- If a bad day is coming, have a fun activity set up after the bad day to keep your mood positive and uplifted.

Gina Beavers
Military Mommy
Virginia, USA

The next survey participant is often overlooked and underappreciated, but has the wisdom, faith and courage to persevere on her own, not by choice, but by destiny. Meet Gina Beaver, married military mom with two teenage girls and a true *Passionpreneur*. In addition to being a mother and wife, she finds time to work full time as an assistant Chief of Staff. One of her greatest passions is setting a continuing education example for her children so they understand the importance of education and how it helps them following their dreams.

1. What does passion mean to you? Was it the same passion you had as a child? What will you teach your child in regards to passion, purpose and getting up after being knocked down?

Passion is the driving force behind all personal and professional aspirations. It provides the motivation to achieve our goals and propels us to continue to push forward towards success.

2. Provide a story about what changed/enhanced/turning point (positive or negative) and how you utilized that moment to become the successful person you are today.

As a graduating high school student headed for college I believed that I would ultimately be successful. Looking back at that time, I realize that my priorities were all over the place during college, as I placed high importance on socializing and not schooling, which ultimately caused an academic dismissal from my university. While I was disappointed and deeply in debt, I still continued focusing on my social circle without truly understanding what was needed to drive me toward success. After a year or so I decided to join the military. I figured maybe the discipline there would help me sort out what was important, ultimately reprioritizing my life.

Shortly after boot camp I met my soon to be husband. After dating for a little bit we got married, and 3 months later I found out I was pregnant with our first child. I was 20. While my priorities were straight, I had no clue the magnitude of time, effort, money and dedication it took to be a great mother.

I decided to leave the military so that our child would have at least one steady parent (one who did not deploy) and go back to school. I attended a technical school and obtained my Microsoft Certified Engineer Degree and shortly thereafter got a contracting job supporting the U.S. Navy. I have since completed a Master's Degree in Information Management Technology, been converted to government civilian as the Assistant Chief of Staff for Communications, Knowledge Management Officer and the Deputy Director of Information Technology, and have continued to move up through the ranks of my organization over the last 13 years.

When I think back to that pivotal moment that redirected my life, I recognize that it is two-fold. It began when I entered the Navy and it was reinforced when I got pregnant with our first daughter. I would have to say that my passion angels followed this redirection, stemming from my own personal drive that had been lost for so long and the dreams I had for our daughter. She ultimately saved my life. While I had many people (mostly family) pushing me to succeed in my younger years, I failed myself as well as them, as I did not see the big picture they were trying to create for me.

I learned the hard way. Paying back $35,000 for my academic failures, having to start my career training over after leaving the military with a small child and little money, putting myself back through school to obtain technical certifications, my Bachelors and ultimately my Masters, and being a loving, supporting and dedicated parent to two wonderful girls. While this was tough, it has become a life lesson I continue to give to our girls in hopes that they will make different choices as they blossom into young adults.

I would say that my way was the hard way. Did it work? Well ultimately, but it wasn't easy. Stay in school, dream big, make decisions that support your aspirations and allow your passion to drive you toward success. Do not let your friends or unfavorable behaviors impede your abilities. Bad days are going to happen, it is inevitable; but your mental state and ability to recognize that good days are around the corner will help to keep you on track. Focus on the positives and make decisions that can improve the negatives. Recognize that some of the negatives are out of your control and they soon will pass.

Family and friends are our lifeline, so use them. Simply taking the time to talk about your issues with someone who has your best interest at heart often helps to resolve them faster. Laugh a lot, even at yourself. It helps to keep the mood light and never ever give up on yourself, if you're not fighting for your success it will take you twice as long to get there.

Gina's Passion Point:
- Children are lifesavers and can change our lives for the better. Making us prioritize our activities.
- One setback will not prevent us from achieving our purpose and success. We just have to keep going.
- Do not let friends or unfavorable behavior impede our abilities.
- Never give up on self; if we are not fighting for success, it will take twice as long to achieve it.
- Make decisions that support our aspirations and allow passion to drive us towards our success.

Message from this chapter: *Though we come from different places in the world, have different professions and maybe a different race we all want to be happy, enjoy our families, make them proud of us and share our journey with them. Passion does not see color, but rather it sees the heart of the individual.*

CHAPTER 7: BE COMPASSIONATE

"Embrace opportunities to be with empathetic people. You'll likely walk away from your time with them feeling warmly embraced in return."
–Grandpa Floyd

This chapter will focus on adding compassion into our passion. I often think of the time when I graduated from high school and working for my mentor at an engineering firm. I approached her and asked about her feeling towards me starting my own business, and her first question was "Why am I starting the business?" I responded, "For money." My mentor shook her head and walked away, I did not understand why but accepted the rejection and proceeded to complete my daily duties.

Later on that day, she shared a story with me. She said, "There was a young man who started his own business and it was very successful. He was young, wealthy and handsome. But he was empty in the inside and when the going got tough he began to panic. He then chased the money inside of his gut feelings and his faith, which eventually forced him to file for bankruptcy and divorce. He made it to the top, but he was not fulfilled and was missing his purpose." From this conversation I understood that I needed to pursue a career that I would not get tired of, makes me happy and gives me a sense of accomplishment once completed.

A part of getting up is to get rid of childish things and emotions. We tend to hold grudges and aggression, bitterness and other depleting characteristics, which may block our blessings. There will always be someone in the world suffering more than us, so be hesitant when we think negative or want to complain, it could be much worst. These stories inspired me and I know they will inspire the readers as well. The stories will include how love conquered obesity, compassion process, takes a village, passion over 9/11, and a widow's fight to regain her strength after her finance is shot three days before Father's Day. Passion can outlive anything. But first we must add some compassion to passion to make it work.

TESTIMONY: TRUE LOVE SEES NO FAULTS

When I think of how long passion survives the test of time, I think of the story of Lee Jordan of Herndon, Virginia. Passion in life is often found when we are genuinely and realistic about life and our weaknesses and fears.

Mr. Jordan was 450 pounds in weight during this period of his life and was in the process of meeting a childhood high school and college sweetheart after 20 years went by and over 250 pounds were gained. His sweetheart, Beth had also had a few changes in her life. She was married, with children, had broken her back from a roller blade accident, and became a personal trainer. But even though they had not talked in 20 years, the two thought of each other and reminisced on the time spent not visioning how the other looks now; it was not a concern when love is involved.

Prior to the meeting at Starbucks, Mr. Jordan was diagnosed with obesity-induced breathing problems, diabetes, and high-cholesterol. His doctors warned him he would die in two years if he did not make a drastic change in his life, but nothing motivated him to change until he met Beth. He thought she would focus her attention on his current weight, but instead had love and encouragement for his newfound lifestyle change and she only saw the old Lee Jordan she fell in love with 20 years prior.

Over the next few months, Mr. Jordan began to take drastic steps to change his life, hiring a personal trainer, inserted a gastric band around his stomach, started a walking program and keeping in constant contact with Beth, who continued to motivate him with a letter or phrases like, "if you show up, you win". Mr. Jordan felt alive again and a functioning part of society with a passion to lose weight, live healthy and self-confidence. Then Beth went through a divorce and the two engaged and married at the same Starbucks they met after being apart for 20 years.

From 454 pounds and a 72-inch waist to weighing 178 pounds and reducing his waist to a size 34, Mr. Jordan and Beth are modern day passion pioneers. Mr. Jordan said it himself; "love, acceptance and encouragement were the difference-makers for him". Today both are ACE-certified personal trainers, run marathons and triathlons together and created a boot camp in Jacksonville, Florida to help women live a healthier life. Passion with love leads to purpose. Every time I'm having a bad day and want to give up, I think of the way these two love birds found life, passion, love and purpose. I will never give up on my dreams thanks to them.

ADD COMPASSION

Passion is in everything. In fact, it is the root of the word compassion. Compassion is the feeling of empathy for others, and the emotions we feel when others are suffering that motivates us to help. My goal today is to put passion and compassion into everything I do, this way I can manage my emotions effectively and help move others with my real life scenarios. What do we do when someone wrongs us? Do we open the door for someone who has slammed the door in our face? Most will not, we live in a society of hurt people, trying to hurt people. I choose to be different and allow the person who has wronged or hurt me, to go free. It takes more energy to plan and think negatively then it does to do something positive for someone.

The reality is others will be offended when we pursue our dreams. When we muster the courage to think outside the box, exceed our own expectation and expect to be the best, others get jealous of this attitude because they wish they had the same ability.

Unfortunately, an inability to control our emotions when the offense occurs (whether external or internal) will cause us to become distracted from our purpose. Compassion is the way to fight bullying in the world today. Not only can compassion help stop bullying it can also rebuild a community.

The opinions of others should never get under our skin because they do not have the fortitude or qualifications to judge us. Never let the opinions of others get in the way of our destiny; the root of their frustration is the key to our success. We must get out of our own way, today.

COMPASSION STEPS

As we look to add compassion in our lives, we need to remember to keep our compassion genuine. To do this we should practice having compassion for our failures, mistakes, and bad decisions. The following steps helped me add compassion into my everyday thinking:

1. ***God's Compassion***-Compassion starts and ends with God. We must learn to forgive ourselves for the bad decisions and mistakes we have made in our lives, as God forgives us. It is a process learned over a course of a person's life, and they may never completely know each lesson until we are on our deathbed. In the meantime we must forgive, love ourselves, and have compassion for who we are now.

2. ***Love with Compassion***-Love with compassion no matter the differences among us. We are all created equal and need to treat others with respect and love. The world should think with love. We need to treat the women of the world the same way we want our daughters and mothers treated. Love is all around us; we need to be receptive to it and not let bitterness from the past linger into our future.

3. *Positivity early*-When we wake up in the morning, we should wake up with nothing but positive thoughts. Down south we call this "waking up on the right side of the bed". To give compassion to others we have to have love for ourselves. If we cannot love the person we are in the morning, it is darn near impossible to love someone else or shed some compassion towards his or her journey. In the morning we should create a motivation phrase for ourselves to remind us of our passion and purpose. My personal message is, "Thank you for waking me up. God you are good; thank you for the wisdom, favor and the Holy Spirit to make this day better than yesterday".

4. *Time to Heal*- Dedicate a specific time period to grieve and release negative emotions. We are humans, there will be bad moments and days in our life, but if we know how to manage our emotions, the damage to the positives in our lives will be minimal. In acting class, we would often yell out, scream, sing and dance to release our inner emotions to connect to the character. When we go through a negative situation and manage our emotions, we not only come out with discipline, but confidence and strength that we can survive anything with patience.

5. *Forgive to live*-Learn how to forgive others who have wronged us. They are going through something we may not be able to understand. We never know a person's complete life story. There are always three sides of the story: their version, your version and God's version (McIntosh Family). Forgive the people who have lied, cheated, tarnished our name and used us, it will help build compassion in ourselves and provides closure. To live we

have to forgive, the burden of bitterness is too heavy to carry. LET IT GO.

6. **Manage Anger-** We need to manage our anger towards people who deserve a piece of our mind. The old saying, "two wrongs don't make a right" is true; we must learn to turn the other cheek to negativity. Growing up, violence was the only answer utilized to resolve conflict but the results did not solve anything, it only increased the problem. Similar to fighting fire with fire, it just keeps spreading; but if we just use water (compromise, communication, common sense) eventually the fire will lose its flame. When people do things to test our patience we must dig deep inside of us and maintain our compassion for people who have wronged us. Karma is a good thing only if we have been good to others.

7. **Only one Judge-.** We must stop judging others and start loving them instead. Compassion will help us stop judging people based on appearance and dialect. I can remember working on the television series The Wire as an extra and looking for the director from HBO, thinking he was going to be dressed in shoes from Italy, a suit custom made for the academy awards. But much to my dismay, I could not find him, so I turned and ask the closest person next to me who resembled a surfer or skateboarder from California. "Excuse me, have you seen the director? I want to see how and what it takes to be a director in Hollywood". The skateboarder stepped back and smiled, then said, "Nice to meet you, extras are not allowed in this area." Life lesson never judge a man by his appearance, judge him by his watch and teeth, because time is important to him and his teeth are important to eating and a great first impression.

8. ***Understanding our pros and cons-***We must take time to understand ourselves. We should engage in thought provoking exercises that stimulate our mental passion. If we don't understand who we are and what we want, how can we expect others too? Understanding our strengths, weaknesses, opportunities and threats in business is called the SWOT analysis.

9. ***Every day perform one good deed-***To continue to receive blessings we must subject ourselves to doing well for others. It is essential to help others learn how to love and live with compassion. The community is dependent on our good deeds, which will be received and reciprocated. If we forget where we come from, we will lose focus on where we are going. We must instill compassion in everything we do, this way we can forgive others and ourselves. The Dalai Lama believes, "If you want others to be happy, practice compassion. If you want to be happy, practice compassion."

10. ***Do not compare to others-***Do not compare the success of others to the success of our lives. If we do this, we often compare our failures to others success. This is a mental roadblock from concentrating on our passion, thinking positive and living with purpose. The only person we need to compare ourselves too is the person we were yesterday and the day before that. Originality will carry us closer to our purpose quicker than copying someone else's happiness. There is no shortcut to finding our passion and living with compassion. When the time is right, our time will come; we have to stay focused and faithful. God will take care of the things out of our control.

11. ***Be thankful*-**Every night before we go to sleep, we should give God thanks for the all the things we enjoyed and endured to create the person we are today. Asking God for understanding and wisdom to help us understand the lessons to be learned. The more good deeds we accumulate over our life the more we are entitled to receive blessings. I am thankful for my failures, rejections and bad decisions, these situations have made me a better person, man, and father. Without the existence of rainy days, I would not appreciate the true beauty of a sunny day.

COMPASSIONEERS

To help better understand the art of living with passion I have included real life stories of people whom have changed my life by enduring their own personal trials and tribulation, facing their fear with integrity and perseverance, letting their passion lead to their purpose and making a difference in the lives of others. The stories include a mentor who changed my life, late great Jimmy Valvano's speech, Martin Luther King and a single mom who face the murder of her fiancée and kept living with compassion to strengthen her children.

"Don't give up because the pain is intense right now. Get on with it, and before long you will find that you have a new vision and a new purpose." **-Oswald Chambers**

TAKES A VILLAGE

The first compassion example is the late great Ted Cook who was very influential to me thinking positive and overcoming adversity in my younger years.

There are some people we meet and forget, but there are some who will live with us forever, Ted was one of those who has gone but will not be forgotten. He had the heart of a champion and supported every idea I had even I though I did not support myself. He was intelligent, articulate and knew how to have fun. In addition, he supported his family, friends, and community. Whenever he was in the room you knew it. He challenged and pushed me to be more than just good, to be great. He never judged anyone from their background or ethnicity; instead he loved and respected them for who they were. He had a way of looking past the weaknesses of others and just focused on maximizing on their strengths.

 The first day I met Mr. Cook I was intimidated; he had a house bigger than my kindergarten school, he knew everyone and they loved him. He would always say, "I do not deserve all the credit, and it takes a village to raise our sons/daughter. A village of the mindset." This saying has stuck with me ever since his death. Ponder the thought; if we have a village of people pursuing their passion in a positive light, we will foster a positive and passionate environment for our kids.

 A kid with a structured household and a since of purpose is a kid destined for greatness, hence his son the starting point guard for the University of Duke. Mr. Cook was a loving man, who loved his wife Jan Cook who is so much like him, full of compassion, positivity, love and purpose. The world needs more parents like the Cooks who set goals for their kids, this way they could see the path forward to success. His son has the same qualities as his dad; wherever he goes he is loved. The passion the Cooks exhibited towards their employees and people in general was full of compassion.

 I share Mr. Cook's story to say, "We don't have to be the smartest, fastest, or strongest to win, we just have to be compassionate about things we do. Spend time developing our passion and everything will work out for a greater good. Our passion will be placed in our hard work and the output will speak for itself." Always remember we all define our personal success differently. It's not about money; it's about competing and completing. Mr. Cook completed me and never complained on a bad day, just smiled and said, "God is good".

INTERVIEW: PASSION OVER MURDER

Think you or your sister is eight months pregnant, found her soul mate, planned their life out and then suddenly the bullet of a stranger's gun changes everything over a few dollars. What do we do next?

The next story will detail how a young single mom used passion and compassion to cope with the loss of her fiancée and best friend. The story is dear to me, he was a childhood friends of mine and never used violence as a remedy but still was subjected to it. This young lady at twenty-five years old and eight months pregnant, life was good then the violence of the streets of Washington D.C. changed her life in a blink of an eye, one day before father's day. How would she make it through? Read her responses feel her passion and commitment to provide the best parent for her daughter's.

The ability to rise and keep going after tragedy is amazing once we get over the hump of pain, sorrow and guilt. The world is not equipped with the answers to certain life changing events, but with faith, purpose and passion we can survive anything. The ability to push through when all is lost is the deepest passion we could ever show, after death, disability or a violent assault.

1. ***What is Passion to you?*** "Passion is striving for betterment and happiness. As a child I was always passionate about helping others and doing my best. I was never a child who expressed, 'I can't do something.' I always made an attempt to try and always worked towards perfecting what was difficult."

2. ***What did you tell your three beautiful girls to help them deal with loss of their father?*** "I told them we are blessed, able, and determined. We can do whatever we put our minds to. We are able. We as a family can move pass anything in life before something tragic happens again."

3. ***How do you prepare for life now?*** "We never know when our day is coming, but we know that day will arrive; so, we must prepare our children how to not only survive, but also survive without us."

4. ***Had you experienced the loss of a loved one before?*** "I had but nothing tragically--all of the sudden. The experience of losing my significant other/the father of my children was unexpected. I was not preparing for death at that moment in my life. We were preparing to celebrate Father's Day the next day and preparing to bring a new life into the world. At the time of my loss I was a mother of an 8 year old, a 1 year old and 8 months pregnant. The first time you ever experience tragedy you say to yourself "WHY ME?" You begin to doubt everything meaningful in your life. Happiness that was granted (what you had access to) has been taken away abruptly."

5. ***How did you manage to get up after this?*** "I went through phases.
    1. One phase -I called it "The Battle of the Mind". It's like you're fighting inner turmoil with the event and trying to accept what happened.
    2. Second Phase-You go through denial----just stuck and it's on repeat in your mind over and over.
    3. Third Phase-You have moments of "what ifs" and you look for anyone to blame.
    4. Fourth Phase-The Emotional Rollercoaster---the phases you go through are all over the place and can be triggered by any reminder.
    5. Fifth Phase-Mourning- the moment you have your ride on the emotional roller coaster. The mourning comes in waves.

6. As all these phases merge together you move closer to acceptance, but you're left feeling empty.

7. ***How did you relax your mind?*** "When your mind is in turmoil you seek a solstice (a turning point). You try to work towards to putting your mind at ease. I lost faith in many things but someone came to my aid, helped me to focus but not dwell. You have to be true to yourself and get yourself to a place where you are not feeling stressed and unable. You have to learn to let go. Nothing is easy but you still have to remain positive. Here's the thing: the strong don't always win and you will face setbacks just like everyone else does. The key is you don't give up. I can't give up. As a reminder to myself to stay strong, I look at my beautiful three daughters who need me. If I am no good, then I am no good to them. I have to keep on keeping on and don't allow my trials & tribulations to set me back."

8. ***Where do you think your passion, motivation or energy came from to go on?*** "Not sure where my passion came from, but it can come from disease, tragedy or setbacks, sometimes in life we have no other choice but to go on because if we don't we will mentally decay in the inside due to the pain and hurt caused by our failures, loses and rejections. We must dig deep during these times of anger and sadness, it is not the bitterness or the aggression that will see us through and help reach the level of maturity and comfort we seek to move forward." I remember losing my aunt and I started questioning God's reasoning for taking my aunt instead of others. As a kid, I thought bad people died first so God could make the world a better place. I was wrong.
9. ***Did you use anything else to help you relax?*** " Other things that helped me work towards putting my mind at ease:
    1. Music
    2. Daily Word and biblical scriptures
    3. Church
    4. Journaling
    5. Talking with others who experienced similar events
    6. Encouraging others gave me strength

Her story was one to remember and to reflect, if we respond with passion we can accomplish anything. Having knowledge and faith gives us peace. We have to let go of the past so we can embrace the future. Sometimes we have to start over, and it's ok. Trust in the season and understand it does get better. I have learned from my experiences we have to face reality in order to receive our destiny.

PASSION OVER 9/11

    Passion by death is not an easy transition, especially if it is often associated with crime, war, and tragic events. Like the single mother who lost her husband it takes great strength and continuous reinforcement to overcome death.

    One of my families' closest childhood friend's fathers was a victim in the September 11th attack on the Pentagon. This was a sad day for my family; I could only imagine how it hurt him and his family. Especially his mother, to go from being a wife to a widow in a matter of seconds is major. She would have to create her life all over again, which in itself needs the "passion of willpower". Willpower will lay dormant in our bodies until it is awakened by a dramatic event. Imagine being at work and then looking at the T.V. and seeing the building your husband works in has just been hit with a plane.

    I could not imagine the pain I would go through if someone called me at work and said my daughter was in Newtown, CT at school and a gunman came in shooting. These events, although horrific, produce the "passion of willpower" in the person, the community, and families. Life does go on and we must lift ourselves up in passion praise and continue our pilgrimage towards happiness. We must learn to grieve and/or fall but at the same time visualize a way forward. Anything is possible with will power, passion and faith.

PASSION OVER STRESS

Negative situations are opportunities waiting to happen but sometimes we need to take the negative perspective out of the situation. Sometimes we can get bombarded and overwhelmed with the problems (negativity), instead of focusing on the solutions (positive) to resolve or improve the situation. When we are in our comfort zone, we need our undivided attention focused on our purpose and passion without distractions.

To find our passion during a stressful situation, we will need to focus on the solution and not the problem to reduce the amount of time and energy placed toward negative people, conversation, and relationships. The negative energy often forces you to think about what, when, why, where, and how. I remember working for a supervisor who did not care for my concepts or me. We knew each other pretty well, I was her boss before and now she has become my boss. At the time, I did not realize that her opinion actually sparked my passion of writing and helped me focus on my purpose in life. I took the negative feedback at work and utilized it to motivate me to move forward with my personal endeavors, which helped me write a book in two months.

If we spend time complaining about what others are not giving us or allowing us to do, we will miss the blessing of having the capability to ascertain things for ourselves. There is nothing in this world we cannot accumulate without sacrifice, determination and passion.

Message from this chapter: *Live with compassion for others and yourself. You will never know when you will need someone and when someone will need you. Treat people better than they treat you and you will always win in the end.*

-SECTION IV: MENTAL PERSPECTIVE-
You are what you think….

CHAPTER 8: MENTAL STABILITY

Psychology is deeply rooted in everything we do whether we want to recognize it or not. This chapter will take a peek at Maslow's approach to self-actualization and how it relates to passion. I agree without Maslow's self-actualization approach because there are similarities in searching and living with passion, fulfillment being the main catalyst. Everything we do will involve some portion of the brain and require some level of thought and focus.

MASLOW'S HIERARCHY OF NEEDS

According to Jen Neitizel, a person cannot follow their passion until they reach the peak of Maslow's hierarchy of needs, self- actualization. What exactly is self-actualization? The best way to describe Abraham Maslow's description of self-actualization is a 20th century man reaching his fullest potential, or as Kendra Cherry stated on Self-actualization refers to the desire for self-fulfillment, namely, to the tendency for him to become actualized in what he/she is potentially. This tendency might be phrased as the desire to become more and more what one is, to become everything that one is capable of becoming." Thus, in order to follow or pursue our passion, we must first meet our needs, and at each stage we will gain confidence to share the things we have learned along the way and maybe some passionate activities we encountered along the way.

Let me walk you through my life and drive towards my passion as the first subject to go through the hierarchy of needs to give you a template to utilize for your personal analysis:

1. **Physiological Needs.** This is the first step in the hierarchy,

which includes the ability to survive such as the need for water, air, food, and sleep. Maslow believed these needs are the most basic and instinctive needs; all needs become secondary until these physiological needs are met.

For myself, I cannot function unless I am sleeping, eating and breathing. I do not know many people who can function well in a day without breathing; as a matter of fact, I don't know any person alive who can do that. For example, I feel awesome before a workout when I eat, drink and sleep right. If I do not get a good amount of sleep, well-balanced meal, and drink water, I become sluggish, moody and my workouts suck! This stage is the foundation for the subsequent stages.

2. **Security Needs.** I call this stage a grown person's dream. According to Maslow, this stage focuses on the need for safety and security. This is the priority of most women in the world. Satisfy the stage and we will be one step closer to our passion Maslow states, "Security needs are important for survival, but they are not as demanding as the physiological needs."

If we are providers for our family our responsibility is to provide a roof, security, and shelter for our family. On the contrary, if we don't have safety and security we will expend more time and energy thinking for our survival with passion. We cannot maximize our passion until we feel safe and secure in the home environment, in relationships and in our careers.

3. **Belonging Needs.** Whether the love we receive from our parents is negative or positive, we will meet people along the way who can change our direction with love and compassion. This love will make us feel needed, which also

ties back to safety and security. As Maslow states, "These needs include the feeling for belonging, love, and affection. Relationships, such as friendships, romantic attachments, and families, help fulfill this need for companionship and acceptance, as does involvement in social, community, or religious groups."

    The art of getting up when knocked down is having the ability to ignore negativity and instead focus on the silver lining of the lesson and how to learn from it. As a Youth basketball coach, my players developed more during a loss versus a win. When faced with adversity and sadness we open ourselves up for self-reflection, self-discovery and self-improvement; losing has a way of humbling us and refocusing our thoughts so we can eventually win.

4. **Esteem Needs.** I call this stage Maslow way of talking about Facebook, Twitter and Instagram. We live in a society full of people looking for social acknowledgement and promotion. According to Maslow this stage focuses on the need for self-esteem, personal worth, social recognition, and accomplishment. Maslow in the 1950's had a vision about what we would end up enduring every day in 2013; we have a society full of children looking for self-esteem, personal worth, societal recognition and success at rates as fast as the speed of the Internet.

    This stage to me is where bullying, sexual abuse & assault, rejection, psychological abuse and coercion handicap most teenagers. We often accept the opinion of a negative person before we can accept a positive response; it is as if we are looking to fail. But when we are looking for passion we must focus on positive thinking and living. My mother would always force me to smile when I was mad which helped me (1) reduce my anger, (2) manage my anger, (3) realize my attitude and (4) scare the person I am mad at. This little mental skill helped me defeat adversity when it entered into my life.

A smile a day can make the pain go away. If we continue to be led by the opinions of strangers in person or online, we lose our self-identity, which is the foundation of our strengths. We need to be assuring of ourselves prior to engaging the community and social networks. When following our passion, self-esteem is crucial to spreading love and compassion to others through mentoring and networking, if we do not feel good about our own work, it will be hard for us to motivate others. In this stage we discover who are our quitters and thoroughbreds.

5. **Self-Actualization Needs.** We made it; we are on the way to changing our life or beginning it by following our passion. Once we have completed and passed each stage of the hierarchy, we have a chance to reflect on our holistic self, growth and awareness of our strengths and weaknesses. Maslow states, "Self-actualizing people are self-aware, concerned with personal growth, less concerned with the opinions of others, and interested in fulfilling their potential.

In a society full of copycats and people replicating everything from pictures to computers we have a select few of individuals who stand out like a sore thumb. According to Maslow, these individuals are doing the most with the potential they have. Once we reach this stage, we are ready to follow our passion.

CHARACTERISTICS OF SELF-ACTUALIZED PEOPLE

After going through each stage of needs, the order may

change and some of our needs may overlap, but, for the most part, the physiological and self-actualization needs will remain the same. When going through our needs, focus on positive thinking only and do not spend too much time and energy on negative aspects of our lives.

In addition, we cannot get wants confused with needs; focus on necessity to reach self-actualization. For the art of getting up is to think positively on our good and bad days. As the great Nelson Mandela stated, "We are the captains of our fate and masters of our soul. "We must realize how strong, smart, and blessed we are to have the opportunity to still breathe, see, walk, talk and feel.

Maslow identified the following characteristics of self-actualized people:

1. **Acceptance and being real:** Self-actualized people are realistic about themselves and the world. They believe it is a waste of time and energy to be anything but ourselves.
2. **Problem centering:** Self-actualized individuals are the problem solvers of the world. They are masters of the 80/20 rule. These individuals are motivated by a sense of personal responsibility and ethics.
3. **Spontaneity:** Self-actualized people are spontaneous in their thoughts and behavior. These individuals are open and unconventional. I am spontaneous so much, that I am often looked at as being weird or different. Self-actualized people are different and will always stand out in the crowd or create a new crowd.
4. **Solitude and Privacy:** Self-actualized people have a need for independence and privacy. In writing this book I spent

numerous hours in Starbucks, Panera Bread, and the library spending quality time with my mind to develop my critical thinking. I enjoy the company of others but when developing I completely shut down. I would always tell my single friends after a split up or separation, "Solitude is not a bad thing; it is a new opportunity for self-discovery and self-actualization. Solitude will often increase your latitude and attitude if managed wisely". Do not be afraid of being alone; instead concentrate on learning ourselves over and over again.

5. **Freshness of Appreciation - Humble Pie:** Self-actualized people tend to view the world with a continual sense of appreciation, wonder and awe. Even simple experiences continue to be a source of inspiration and pleasure. To appreciate the simple things in life we need to fall in love with every day as if we have been reborn and it is a new day.

6. **Peak Experiences:** According to Maslow, individuals who are self-actualized often have *peak experiences*, or moments of intense joy, wonder, awe and ecstasy. After going to Africa I felt an increase in significance, fulfillment and spirituality.
   - **Significance:** I felt an increase in personal awareness and understanding as a man, American, and human being. It was a significant turning point in my perspective of the world and my life.
   - **Fulfillment:** The feelings and emotions generated from my trip cannot be described by mere words; the opportunity was priceless and intrinsically rewarding. I have been to places people dream about or only get the chance to visit after a long career of continuous working.
   - **Spiritual:** It is as if God has a bigger plan for my

life and I am a messenger for his work. Passionpreneurs are not fulfilled by personal accomplishments; they need a little more out of life. We are looking to inspire and uplift others by any means necessary, putting our reputation on the line to improve the lives of our community's children's children.

7. **Sense of Humor**: According to Maslow "self-actualized people have a thoughtful sense of humor" and with an awesome sense of humor we become magnets to other people. I love and live to laugh and make others laugh whether it is in the midst of adversity or happiness. Passionpreneurs are able to enjoy the humor in situations and laugh at themselves.

PASSION PYRAMID
"It is not just levels to this, its morals and values as well"
Oumar Hill

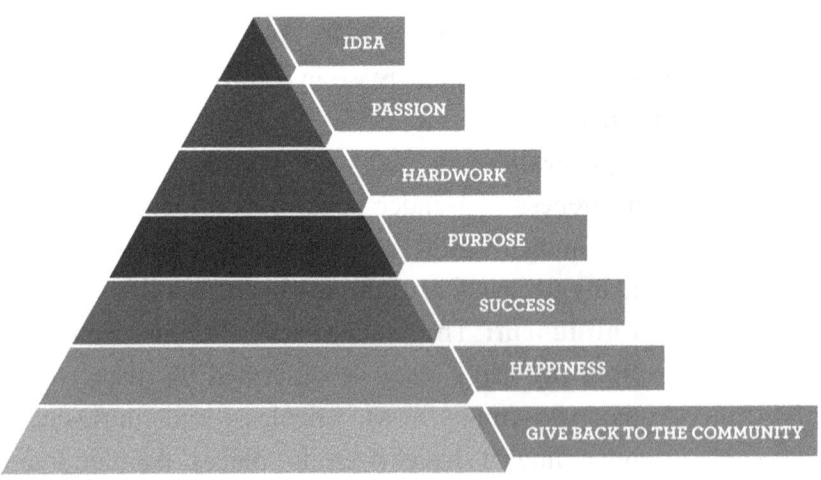

All of the levels above coupled together equals fulfillment with one's self. The ultimate goal for most people is to live a life of fulfillment and/or a career, which brings fulfillment as well. This pyramid approach is stating everything starts with an idea, followed by choices, our drive, perseverance, and the purpose of our passion. Then we begin to move towards happiness and success mentally because we are doing something we love doing and we have a passion for regardless of the success measured by others.

The happiness and success levels once satisfied by our own actions lead to the last stage, which leads to Self-fulfillment. Like building a house, we need a strong base. If your purpose in life is unknown, this is okay, just follow your dreams, work hard and God will lead you to your purpose. Passions should be in everything you do; this includes your career, leisure activities, family, relationships and educational endeavors. .

Like most things in life, passion has many levels to it and there are certain things we must do to make sure we make it to the next level. The goal for the pyramid is to find self-fulfillment after we have taken a step towards our purpose in life. I have the greatest satisfaction of speaking to kids from the boys and girls club I participated in as a youth, Oxon Hill Boys and Girls Club. This gives me some self-fulfillment because I am able to share my testimony with children that are more than likely going through the same problems I did as a kid. We share a bound because of the environment and elements within that particular environment.

The pyramid is designed to reiterate the importance of following your passion is to live a life of fulfillment and help others reach their passion as well. Below are the details of each level within the passion pyramid:

LEVEL 1- IDEA

This is where we have been thinking of doing something different or changing our surroundings. We begin to picture ourselves in a different career or light. During this time we are gathering thoughts and wishes. This is where our dreams are captivating our mind with the possibility of living the life we cannot wait to live and being happy. For myself, I had been writing minutes for doctors, scientist and government agencies for years and published them amongst the organization, but never authored my own book. My thoughts were consumed with the HOW can I make this a reality, WHEN should I start the process, and WHAT should I write about? All these questions were strengthening the idea to motivate others. Passion and purpose are not the focus here; it is more about getting started.

During this stage we are learning how to function within our passion, but our ideas will continue to grow after this level. The next level is where we focus more on our passion.

LEVEL 2-PASSION

The choices we make in life often determine our future. Every student in high school and college should understand the choices made today would be paid in adulthood. It may not seem damaging or rewarding today but choices are like seeds, we have to water them before we notice results. During our passion journey we will make choices regarding our environment, friends, social activity and interest. These choices will coincide with our passion and purpose. We will do more things, which are directed towards our passion.

Thinking is a major part of this stage and we may experience doubt as we collect additional information regarding our passion. The choice we make during our passion journey will determine if we are successful or not with regards to reaching the next level, which is passion. We have to be extra careful of the people we consult with to answer our questions and lead us towards our passion. This will increase or decrease our workload and our time to reach our passion.

We have to do a lot of homework when it comes to making our dreams a reality or overcoming a traumatic event in our life. Others will be able to provide their best advice but ultimately we have to make decisions for the better of our own purpose.

LEVEL 3-HARDWORK

Now it is time to expand on the idea and explore our passion ideas. We have more answers to the questions in the previous level and it is time to walk towards our passion. We have to take the walk from the first level and lead with our actions. For me, with the book, I started to reach out to authors, think about marketing strategies, and consulted mentors and took other actions, which will put me closer to the realization of achieving my passion. During the time I am answering my doubts, and the questions I have regarding my passion, I am simultaneously building self-esteem and confidence in my craft.

This level is critical and important to making sure the pyramid does not fail. During this time we give clear and detailed information to others of our dreams and admirations. This level is where all the hard work, long hours and commitment is implemented. If our passion is not strong it will be revealed during this level.

This level will determine if we like what we are doing or if we love it. This is where passion angels come into our life and begin to plant seeds. We come out of this level with a better understanding of our passion and lean closer to our purpose.

LEVEL 4-PURPOSE

In this level we try to determine if what we learned in the passion level. The passion level is the combination of ideas and concepts coming from our families, friends, colleagues and TV, but now we have to determine what the truth versus hype is for ourselves. What is the ultimate reason we are doing the things we are doing and why are we here? We begin to take an intellectual dive into why we pursuing our dreams and who this is affecting.

My purpose to share stories, testimonies, and real life situation is to assist other people throughout the world that are going through the same problems. The idea of our passion is minor compared to the bigger picture, which is our purpose in life. Purpose includes everything from the concept of a thought to the intangible skills developed along the way to building confidence in our passion and becoming happiness in all facets of life.

During this level we begin to look back on the things we have experienced during our journey and what they meant to us during and after the event occurred. When things happen in our life, we do not have a chance to see what's next to come until we keep going forward. Only then do we comprehend the true meaning of the action and why it happened. Understanding things happen the way they do, purposeful thinking and analysis of our journey. As I created the book, I would send out Facebook status updates with pieces from the book to share with my family and friends, not only did I get a ton of likes but I received constructive feedback and communication to help me structure the content within the book.

Often purpose is bigger than what we think it is and we do not have any control over our purpose in life. Your goal in life is to live with and follow your passion and dreams to define and determine your purpose. Everything else is icing on the cake.

Now people ask this all the time, "How do I find my purpose?" I honestly wish it were a simple answer like, but it's not. My personal opinion about finding purpose totally depends on the individual, have they matured during the trials of life and if they are mentally ready for the next level. Purpose will be found through our maturity, passion, conviction and lessons learned. My purpose to inform, enrich and uplift humanity by any means necessary has trickled into my professional career and leisure activities.

When we lead with passion it will spread throughout everything we do in our life. A key to knowing if we are headed in the right direction is our gut feeling, it gives us a sense of fulfillment or not. A purpose driven life is a life full of meaning and contentment. Living with purpose is infectious.

LEVEL 5- SUCCESS

I call this section the art of getting up. With the pursuit of passion or following your passion you will be challenged, rejected, delayed, and doubtful, but with the fortitude to keep the faith and to keep pushing we will eventually reach our purpose. This is where we find success with perseverance and persistence. The only way this pendulum swings in the positive direction is with a "no quit' attitude, not taking no for an answer, pushing through when others give up, staying the course when the path is not clear, and having a faith in our vision and purpose.

In high school I was exceptional athlete but an average student, C plus average struggling to learn Spanish 2. Now I am, a world traveler, learning and speaking multiple languages. Who would have thought? Anything is possible with hard work, determination and a "no quit" attitude, God placed me in a position to be successful, be a blessing to others and my life can serve as a testimony for others. There have been many times in my life when I wanted to throw in my hand and just walk away, but I could never walk away from my community, parents, and colleagues who have helped me become the man I am today.

In order to reach the next level, which is happiness, we must endure negative events to learn from them and this will help us enjoy the happiness we will experience on the next level. If we lose confidence or take a pause for the cause during this phase, we will lose focus of the passion journey and begin the process all over again as doubt begins to set in. When we encounter difficult times, we should have a community of friends, resources, and relaxing techniques to help us stay on schedule with reaching our dreams. Success is about not giving up and finishing your goals with intensity and confidence.

LEVEL 6-HAPPINESS

Happiness for one person can easily change a few weeks or years later. Happiness is what a person feels inside over a goal they set out to accomplish. To achieve internal fulfillment, we have to come up with an idea and then determine the steps forward and overcome the obstacles in our way to prevent us from success. Think of how far we have come and we will instantly be full of joy and happiness. It is time to celebrate our journey; we have reached a level that very few people muster up the energy to try to obtain. We are doing something we love and we are moving closer to fulfilling our purpose. When we are happy in our career it will spread throughout our personal relationships with our families and friends.

Happiness is addictive and spreads like wild fire. Now the happiness level does not mean we stop working and party our life away, this phase means we begin to perfect our craft in preparation for entrance into our passion zone. The extra work and time spent to pursue our passion becomes fulfilling and we begin to become happy with the extra time spent working towards our dreams and desires. We are happy with the person we are becoming, the things we are doing and will be doing in the future and we are happy about the effect we are having on the lives of others if applicable. We will focus on perfecting our craft during this level so we can be primed for success in our passion zone.

LEVEL 7-GIVING BACK

Self-fulfillment is a bringing of oneself to flourishing completion, an unfolding of what is strongest or best in one's self, so that it represents the successful culmination of one's aspirations or potentialities. In this way self-fulfillment betokens a life well lived, a life that is deeply satisfying, fruitful, and worthwhile. It is diametrically opposed not only to such other reflexive relations as self-defeat, self-frustration, self-alienation, and self-destruction, but also to invasions whereby such injuries are inflicted by forces external to the self.

Cultures around the world have regarded self-fulfillment as the ultimate goal of human striving and as the fundamental test of the goodness of a human life. Once we find a career we love, and then begin to give back by helping others reach their goals and then consistently make better positive choices, success is inevitable.

Message from this chapter: *Your mind is the most important muscle in your body, continue to develop it and prosper from your mental growth.*

CHAPTER 10: PASSION LIFE CYCLE

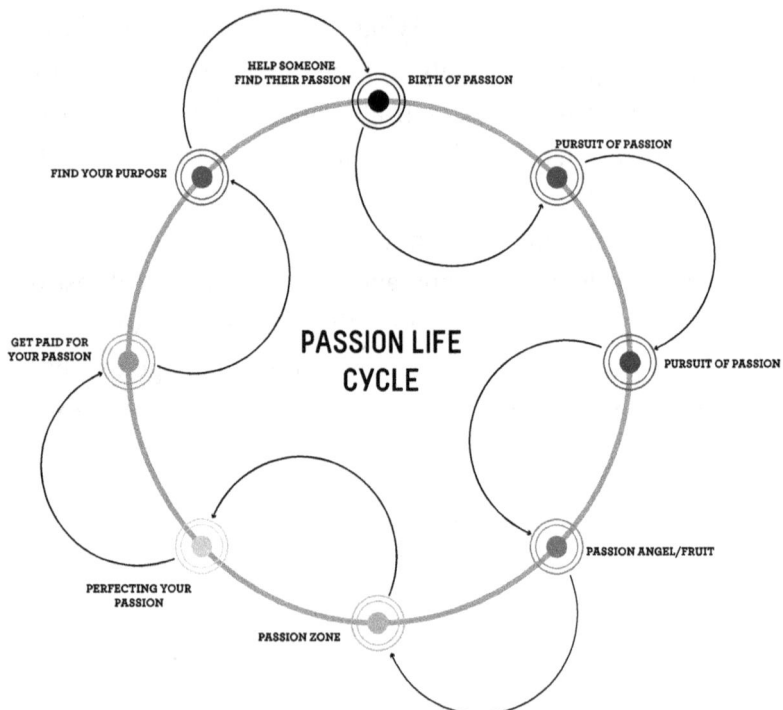

In this chapter we will take a look into my experience with finding my passions and the cycle of events I went through to discover the things I love to do. My cycle is not a scientific proven research project but more of an individual capturing the key things, which made a difference in my life. We all have various ideas of what we have to do to reach our passion but this is a foundation of our passion life cycle.

A passion life cycle is a series of stages through which my passion passes during its existence. The stages are flexible and are in order according to my experiences in my life. Each reader will have to determine where he or she is on the life cycle from a personal, career, relationship and spiritual standpoint. Passion is person specific. The goal here is to provide a foundation for our passion and then build upon this foundation. Visit www.passionwith-in.com for additional information on the passion life cycle, which can be found within the passion workbook.

STAGE 1-BIRTH

Passion is birthed from an internal desire to seek a life of fulfillment and mental satisfaction. During this stage I began to discover what I liked and what I really wanted to do. I also discovered what I did not want to do, which helped me focus on the things I wanted to do. This stage is the moment in my life where I found a new beginning in search of something internally fulfilling. The core of my decision-making is done at this stage and it incorporates all the information collected from the forest of life's research and analysis.

This stage can be as short as a week or as long as a decade; it depends on the individual and how focused and serious he (or she) is about following his (or her) passion. This could be the birth of an idea towards our career change, personal relationship or spirituality. Birth of our passion is where we open our minds up to possibility and dreams.

STAGE 2-PURSUIT

After the birth stage, I became curious and investigated the likeliness of fulfilling my passion. Is this what I really want to do? Am I too old or too young? I'm sure I could have come up with additional questions, but my point is doubt is involved when we pursue our dreams because it is something new. However, I faced my doubt with self-esteem and faith, which helped me develop my confidence in my journey. This is where I first began to build confidence and self-discipline methods to give myself structure. In addition, this stage I conducted research, analyses, and networking with individuals who were currently in the career field I desired to get into. I began to read about motivational speakers, listen to their speeches, and write my own, I had started my transition from a 9-5 to working for myself.

Immediate change happens when we are financially well off or have a spouse that supports our career change and passion and will accept the financial responsibility of the household. This change means we can quit our job, and spend 100% of our time following passion. This stage is a perfect opportunity to change our current way of life and bring happiness to others in our life. The value of two is always better than one, especially if we have someone who believes in us and pushes us to do the things, which make us happy.

Gradual change is for the type of person whom maintains their current job and works on their passion in their leisure time. The individual will still be a big contributor within the family both financially and mentally. This change will take frequent communication within the family during the pursuit to sustain the families' current lifestyle. Risk is very low here and it allows the person exploring their passion the opportunity to change their mind or reevaluate their passion.

The slow motion stage involves more than a change in financial stability; this change is due to death, divorce, catastrophic event, or serious illness. Imagine being married for ten years to a man of your dreams with children and a nice house with a comfortable lifestyle and its Christmas. You leave out of the house and your cell phone rings. It's the state trooper calling you to inform you a drunk driver has killed your family. In these types of situations, there is no immediate fix; gradual in some cases, but the majority takes time to heal mentally, physically and spiritually. We have no choice but to stand up with passion, faith and purpose. During this time we begin to create our passion plan, which is simply a plan that maps out the how and when we plan on achieving our passion goals.

STAGE 3-NEGATIVE FEEDBACK

How I love some good ole fashion negative vibes. After years of people telling me I was not smart enough, strong enough or passionate enough to motivate others, I have learned to turn negative feedback into positive momentum. I believe having a thick skin assisted with my ability to overcome negativity as well. Some inflict some distractions, while others are self-inflicted from our beliefs, upbringing and social life.

This stage could be nicknamed "the life or death" of your passion. Most passions are murdered in this stage due to insecurity, lack of self-discipline, poor originality and listening to everyone else in our life except ourselves. We tend to want to satisfy everyone else before we think about satisfying ourselves. But with negative comes the positive. We need to be able to deflect negativity and turn into a positive motivation. This stage is a building block for turning a negative energy into a positive energy.

As a kid I was obese but I loved to play football. I played as a lineman for years, and I was pretty good. I remembered being teased about my weight but I never let it get to me and used my weight to push others around. My last game of the season I was determined to show the crowd how good I was, I recorded 4 sacks and then capped it off with an 85-yard interception ran back for a touchdown. So, when I turned 13 years old, I was determined to be a running back; besides, the girls really liked them. I told my dad, "Hey I'm going to be a running back one day". He kindly responded, "Boy you can barely run". Mind you my dad has always been tough and expected nothing but the best from me in everything I did, but he always told me I could be anything in life and I was going to be great, so his negative comment was a challenge to me.

I had to take my dad's opinion for face values.

First Question Was he telling the truth? Could I actually run? Is this possible or am I dreaming? **Second Question:** I began to look at people who were in the position and compared how they ran to how I ran. **Third Question**: I realized my dad's, negative criticism had merit and I could run. My running form was not the best, so I began to watch sprinters and professional athletes, how they cut and held their arms. I recorded the videos and replayed them over and over again, then practiced the moments in the mirror before I headed outside to practice more. I was determined to change my father's perspective. I begged my mother to enroll me in track and soccer. I was focused on transforming a negative comment into an opportunity and I used it to better my understanding of the game. After learning how to run, I began playing high school football and my first game starting as fullback I ran for 165 yards and three touchdowns by half time. My dad was so happy and said, "where did you learn how to run like that?" I kindly responded, "I learned from listening to you." ☺

STAGE 4- PASSION FRUIT & PASSION ANGELS

I believe in angels and fruit is the main part of my diet. Each played a key role in my development and maturity as a man. But there are some really awesome people who grace our life and we should keep these individuals in our life.

I have been blessed to have great parents, siblings, friends, classmates and a loving community in Prince George's County Maryland and the District of Columbia. In a world full of hate and deceit, it is refreshing to have honest people in our corner to push us to our fullest potential. Everything happens for a reason. We all have a role to play and we are purposefully placed with a variety of people, some good and bad.

Passion angels and fruits are things, which propel us closer to our purpose in life on purpose or accidentally. Passion angel will keep us on the right direction and keep our perspective on the goal. Passion fruit will help give us knowledge, resources and tools to satisfy our appetite for success. They get us in the zone and allow us the opportunity to grow into our own and we can begin to relax in our passion zone. These are the people we will most likely never forget in our life and who have had the biggest impact on our existence. In this stage we will focus on differentiating the angels from the regular people in our life.

When I was about to give up on myself, passion angels flew in and saved the day. There will be times where our faith and commitment will be tested; we need to make sure our circles of friends are passionate about being our friends. I would have never developed my self-esteem and self-confidence if it had not been for the passion angels who watched over me and prayed for my success. Passion Angels are equivalent to a navigation system in a vehicle; they lead us in the right direction, avoid roadblocks, let us know if we have strayed off the path and slow us down if we are going too fast.

PASSION FRUIT

When I think of fruit, I think of my favorite -- mangoes!!! Somehow this precious fruit always changes my moods. When I eat a mango, it is as if the world stopped and the only thing moving is my mouth and the juice from the mango after I take my first bite. This led me to the development of the "passion fruit" concept; words that help us stay encouraged and motivated to follow our dreams.

My mother is a passion angel who would drop passion fruit every day of my life, "Go to school", "Do your best", "Never give up" and "God is good". These pieces of fruit will sound like confirmation to our journey and will always be on time, if we are open to receiving the information. Think of passion fruit as our best friend helping us get through a bad break up, nothing but positive influence and persistence to keep going and pursue happiness. Not understanding the effect they would have on my life, purpose and passion, these words changed my life; they gave me a little boost every now and again, which is needed to achieve our passion.

This passion fruit has lingered with me throughout my life and has helped me get through tough periods in my life. I can remember my elementary teacher Mrs. Knight yelling at me, "Oumar! Oumar! Come here now" grabs me by the arm and says, "One day you are going to be a leader, just not today". Those moments have stuck with me forever, I knew I was going to be a leader because Mrs. Knight said I was after she spanked me with the ruler a few time, but she gave me the confirmation my family had already bestowed upon my journey.

The road to living with passion is a long road filled with bumps, but if we surround ourselves with positive and passionate friends, whom continuously inject positive vibes and affirmation in our minds, we can get through anything. As Joel Olsten stated on his television show, "We must surround ourselves with positive people, lifters who can lift us up and not pull us down". In addition, fruit when consumed gives us energy and changes our mood because we are happy and fulfilled. Passion cannot be contained; if we encounter a negative spirit we should remove ourselves from the equation, negativity is contagious. We are whom we associate with daily.

PASSION ANGELS

If passion fruit is the fuel for a car then passion angels are the navigation system in the car. When the car drives, it uses fuel to move forward but needs the navigation system to direct us to our destination. Without navigation we would be stuck with following the directions of a stranger or reading a piece of paper while driving. If we don't have *passion angels* in our life to push, motivate, lead and teach us along the way, our journey will be extended.

This group of special individuals reduces the time it takes to find success, passion and love. To fly above the stress, rejection and hatred in the world, we need wings and the support, comfort and unconditional love provided from these special people who give us wings to fly high above the clouds. We all were created for a specific reason, it is easy to quit but it takes passion, guts and courage to keep fighting for our dreams. Having passion angels in our corner is a blessing and they make our journey worth it.

    My first passion angel is my late aunt Gertrude. Her courage, spirit, stature, and values have stayed with me throughout my entire life. I was only graced with her presence for 14 years and it was the best 14 years of my life, full of passion fruit. Taken away too soon by cancer, her soul lives within me; she has instilled passion within me as young man. She was strong mentally, educated, career driven, gave the worst spankings, and could bake the best pie. I feared her beatings more than my parents and loved her cooking more than my parents.

    I remember when I was acting up as a typical teenager, my parents sent me to stay with my aunt for the weekend. My aunt was extra excited to see me and baked a cake which I could smell as I walked in her front door, I was in heaven. My aunt was normal, greeted me with a hug and a kiss. We all sat down and began to have family dinner. I remember the day as if it was yesterday, I was eating meat loaf and my aunt asked, "How are you doing in school?" I replied, "Fine!" Before I knew anything, it was as if she was superman and flew across the table before I could get my next bite of meatloaf. Though she was the youngest of my aunts and uncles, she was the strongest and she was not afraid to show me.

    After the spanking, she took me in the kitchen and had an honest discussion about life, hanging with the wrong people, making better decisions and being a leader. Her discussions have helped me navigate through life in Washington DC during the bad times as a teenager and helped me deal with inequality and professionalism within my career field. My Aunt taught me there is a time to play and there is a time to be professional in the classroom and at home. I only knew her 14yrs of my life, but passion angels don't need a lifetime to change or affect your life.

Passion angels lead by example; they not only talk the talk, but they walk the walk. My aunt was in her twenties when she died but had worked as a news anchor, went to George Washington University and graduated top of her class, and was just a great person. She demanded respect; and was a replica of my grandmother from Greenwood, SC. I have so many positive people in my life who have helped me survive and flourish along the way, but my aunt created me into the man I am today. She is my favorite passion angel and I thought I needed her physically but the effect she had on me mentally last forever.

Only reading stories about NBA and NFL, which have lost millions of dollars, did I find this story of a passion angel in the life of Donald Driver. The article on former NFL star wide receiver Donald Driver was about him being placed on the right path in life by a neighbor. Someone who could have turned their back and just walk away from him, but instead his passion angel provided love and direction, which would ultimately change the life and destiny of Mr. Driver.

In Mr. Driver's younger days, he was running the streets, stealing cars, and selling drugs until he ran into an elderly woman's vehicle with his stolen vehicle. Something inside of him instilled by his father's teachings forced him to check on the senior citizen instead of running from the scene even though the police were in hot pursuit. He stayed and the passion angel told Mr. Driver to go sit on the porch as she told the police the man that hit her ran down the street. She protected him and took him in the house as if he was her own son, lecturing him about right and wrong and caring for his future. This is missing in the world we live in today. Then she did something, which is rarely heard in this day and age, she took it upon herself to counsel and mentor Mr. Driver through questions and answers. Her unconditional love would serve as the love Mr. Driver needed to prevent him from going to jail, but instead going straight to the NFL. The love and compassion she displayed personified the old belief, "it takes a village to raise a child". Mr. Driver has stated in the article, he "did not want to let Miss Johnson down, she was my real grandmother". He felt this way after she died, which is the same effect my aunt had on me. There is not a timeline or specific age where passion angels will be introduced in your life, but when they do make their presence known in your life, don't be afraid of the lesson to be learned.

STAGE 5-PASSION ZONE

After the birth, research, negative feedback and positive reinforcement, we arrive at our passion zone. Now we are ready to take major steps towards changing our life, we have the confidence, created a plan and now it's time to implement. For example while writing this book, I decided to send the draft version to a local editor just to get some feedback. One of the editors said, "You are in the zone" and I was in a zone, my passion zone.

The passion zone takes focus, prioritization, discipline, courage, independence, fortitude and self-stimulation. When I think of my own passion zone, I think of a moment when we truly start to believe in our purpose and ourselves. This is the moment we become encompassed in our passion and self-esteem.

For a person going through anything traumatic, this is the moment when life gets back to normal again. We have to take life one day at a time and not rush the healing process. When we are suffering, learn to appreciate the pain and celebrate. Good days are on the way because troubles do not last always. Healing is a big part of a person who has been hurt or abused. Take time to heal and get up stronger.

The art to getting up is knowing when and how to get up.

Often times we rush coming back from an injury as athletes. Think of the Redskins quarterback Robert Griffin III (RG3) who came back in 2012-13 season from a knee injury mid-season to lead the Redskins to a seven game win streak but in the playoffs he reinjured his knee again putting him out even longer from his injuries. When we rush the healing process we subject ourselves to being hurt again, take our time to heal and get up stronger than ever! Greatness needs time to heal and regain strength to prepare for battle.

STAGE 6-PERFECTING PASSION

Once we reach our passion zone and gain confidence, we must perfect our craft. One day I was riding with my dad near my home in search for kids to play basketball on our team; we needed two additional players to meet the league minimum. While driving, we came across a tall kid. My dad asked him, "Can you play basketball?" He responded, "Yeah!" My dad asked, "Have you played organized basketball?" He said, "No sir". My dad said, "Okay, ride with us to the park down the street and you can play my son." Now even though I had been trained since I was 8 years old by my dad, this kid had God-given talent within him that you cannot measure or define as children. He beat me fair and square; I thought I knew little nuances of the game, but he was by far a superior athlete at the time. This same young man would later on in life win a scholarship to play for Georgetown University. The day he played me, he was clearly in his passion zone and once he received training from my dad, his high school and college coaches, he began to perfect his craft even more, which eventually led him to the next stage, which is getting paid for your passion.

Now for someone going through a life-changing event, this stage means finding your repetition. This means it is necessary to keep doing positive things so they become habit forming, but keep it simple practice, practice, and practice. My motto is practice makes perfect and practice is worth it. If the individual is going through a divorce, this is the moment they will learn how to be themselves again, take it back to what made them happy, stay around the friends who make us smile and stay away from negative people. We need to continuously surround ourselves with positive people.

STAGE 7- GET PAID FOR YOUR PASSION

Some people begin this stage simultaneously with the passion zone, but some don't begin this stage until the last stage of finding our purpose. This is just a friendly reminder that one of the benefits from finding our passion after we begin perfecting it, we will eventually get rewarded for our efforts. Now getting paid for our passion is bigger than any financial reward; it involves getting paid with eternal joy, happiness, smiling and non-stop laughing. These drives will then increase our confidence, self-assurance, wisdom, self-esteem and faith.

For me the reward is God giving me the opportunity to change people's lives by sharing my life and how I overcame my trials and tribulations. When I started my nonprofit to help high school basketball players in the Washington, D.C. area to teach young men about the different challenges in life, college prep and becoming a man, it was life altering. Now, I love to turn on the TV or go to college basketball games and say, "That's my kid!" The ability to see them run up and down the court with millions of people watching and supporting them makes me smile. But it is the life long relationship, which makes me melt inside. The fact I could come back and share my stories with young men who were 2 years old when I was 18 years old and have a concrete effect on their life is amazing. Not only did I help the boys I mentored but also in return they helped me understand the thought process of a teenager, things to be aware of, and how to prepare my daughter for young men soon to come.

How to turn a passion into money

How do I turn my passion into my career? The answer depends on the person asking the question. How soon are we willing to make a change? How focused are we? Think the first step of turning our passion into money is to find a need and fill it with a service. Put the financial reward on the back end and focus on satisfying a need with our skill sets. If we perform a task with passion and effort we will exceed expectations and reward will be sure to come. Then we need to conduct research, talk to people and focus on filling needs. Search for the pros and cons and develop a plan of action. We need to take what we have learned in perfecting our craft and create services to satisfy those needs. Focus on the things that make us happy, listen and consult our parents and close friends and ask them what they think about our endeavors. Let's imagine we are still in college and exploring the idea of following our passion and not what our colleagues are doing.

If we are still in college we have two options; first, we can look at other degrees we may extend our stay at college or we can finish school and use the degree as a validation certification and look for more ways to develop our skill sets. I think college students should explore the possibility to open their own business and look for entrepreneur opportunity. Invest all of our money into our passion before we invest in other things. Stay focused and always remember everything that glitters is not gold. I would suggest working as an intern somewhere with a company we could gain knowledge and experience. Be aware of the sharks in the water and we must guard our dreams with a passion.

If above the age of 30 years old, I assume the person has been working for at least five years and had a sudden change of heart, don't feel fulfilled or don't feel their skills are being maximized. I would suggest creating a transition plan. This is a short plan of how the person plans to transition their current skills into the new job and how to make the same income without falling behind on bills. Next sit down and talk to family members or spouse tell them our intentions and get their feedback. We need to include the important people in our life in the important decision in our life.

If we are going through a traumatic event I would suggest finding the love for ourselves first and then looking for our passion. Often these situations will never be forgotten and can either build us up or break us down. Passion is all about building and uplifting, so let passion be our guide. I would suggest healing and finding closure whether it is in the form of forgiveness or a moment to cry. Once healing has begun, look for opportunities, which will bring us big internal rewards, and the opportunity to share our story with the community to help someone else going through the same situation. My best speeches have been the ones where I can relate to the people who I am speaking in front of, it's like a family affair. People are more inclined to share their troubles with us, if we open up and share our victories and failures with them. Realize once we find our passion, we will be on the road to happiness, success and stability mentally. Trouble does not last always and tomorrow is a new day.

STAGE 8-FIND YOUR PURPOSE

We have discovered something within us and now we have created a plan to work towards changing our life and our vision has become clear. We are on the road to success and we have passion taking us there while being navigated by passion angels. Now we can talk about purpose! We can look back and understand why certain things happened and we did not know why. Things start to make sense, especially our bad days. They were preparing us for this moment. Purpose gives us the feeling of fulfillment and being part of something bigger than ourselves. During our walk in life we will meet two types of people, people who need something from us or people we need something from. We attract both to us from following our passion and we will push others who are unproductive away because we are focused. Purpose gives me a sense of everlasting happiness, legacy and love for generational happiness.

Some people never get the chance to experience their purpose and it's considered a blessing to obtain this opportunity. We should think, live and work with purpose and not just wants. A purposeful life is actually living right and living with a meaning. Purpose is hard to find but once we find it, we are rarely distracted and deterred. Once we follow our passion our purpose is sure to follow.

STAGE 9-HELP SOMEONE FIND THEIR PASSION

Giving back is the most important step in the life cycle and it is often overlooked. The ability to give back to the community is a blessing and honor. To help fight against the bad things in the neighborhood, we need to unite as one again. Society needs the successful or educated members from the community to focus on doing due diligence and providing resources within the community without taking advantage of the community. The best way to spread word of our success is to do something good within the community. Passionpreneurs believe in giving back to the community and without expectations of received funds from the community.

I have dedicated my life to giving back to the children not only within my community, but also in other countries who are in need of motivation and inspiration. Other's needs have helped me overcome my own fears and insecurities. When we give back to our community, we receive a check within our hearts and it stays with us forever. I believe in karma and the things we have done unto others will be reciprocated back in our lives in some fashion or in our children's lives. Following our passion is a life long journey, which is longer than just the life of a job or task.

The people within the community are looking for hope and every time they turn around there goes another politician or leader being escorted to jail for some type of illegal activity. I can imagine the conversations parents are having with their children about voting and why they voted for a person who steals from the people. When we help others, we actually heal ourselves, and like practicing our craft, we are practicing and making sure we don't fall back into the misery pit of sorrow.

Message from this chapter: *You have to find out what your life cycle is and determine which works best for you. Think with purpose and then live with it.*

CHAPTER 11: AUTHOR'S TESTIMONY

MOTHER'S STRENGTH

After witnessing my mother fight her battle with brain cancer, it moved me to want more from myself. I consider my mother a champion because she has served others for years as a nurse, and still managed to have the courage to serve herself. Not to mention she assisted with various HIV and cancer campaigns, and helps with local political campaigns. Without her energy and spirit, I would have never been able to become the man I am today.

"God knows the pain of losing a beloved son; he understands and grieves with us." –Linda Hill

Great parents will not lead their kids in the wrong direction, no matter what. They will give them a template on how to succeed and let the child have an opportunity to decide which positive direction they want to go. My mother is one of the nicest human beings a person could meet, she will literally give a person the shirt off her back and mine, just to make sure that person is clothed and fed. It was a normal day and I was preparing to head back to college and my parents were headed to work. My father was up to his usual king routine, master of the bathroom, prince of the bacon and ruler of the radio. I greeted my mom with a good morning and she returned the favor by yelling, "Clean your room".

This day my mother had a routine doctor's visit at the hospital she worked for. As we departed for school, my mother stated that we should pray for her. Thinking the visit was only because of the high pollen concentration, I did not think much of her statement, but I prayed for her anyways. Thank God she went in for a visit; the doctor determined the sinus problems were not a result of her sinuses, but it was brain fluid draining from her nose.

The doctor knew something was not right and so did my mother. The visit would not only save my mother's life, but it gave me purpose in my life.

My mother was informed her brain fluid was flowing down out of the nose. She needed to have emergency surgery and her time was limited, the drainage had been leaking fluid for a week now.

At that time, I was in my first class and clowning around with my friends, when my phone rings, it's my brother saying, "Get out of class we have to head to the hospital, mom is in the hospital." I am thinking she is at the hospital, not in the hospital. Maybe he forgot she had a doctor's appointment. The phone rings again and it's my dad this time. My dad is a strong man, very physically fit and always a respectable man. I have never seen him in a vulnerable position, but his voice on the phone sounded different because he was in pain.

I ran out of the classroom not sure what to expect when I reached the hospital. Something inside me suggested the worst case scenario, so I ran red lights, put my hazard lights on, and put the pedal to the metal; it was something in my dad's voice that moved me. As I looked back to the day, I realized the value of life and our parents are very important and we should tell them how we feel about them every chance we get; we will never know when judgment day comes.

ARRIVING AT HOSPITAL

My mother was famous for hiding the truth from us to protect us and because she did not want us to worry, but today we all were worried. My mother was diagnosed with a rare condition in which the bone in the nose has deteriorated; this bone prevents the brain from coming out of the nose. Now, if I were in the same situation as my mother, I would have been in trouble. I may have missed my appointment, told the doctor he was crazy and demanded a second opinion. But something about the strength of a woman propelled my mother knew to go through with the surgery, basically by herself.

Greeted at the hospital by my brother and father, I was informed of the details and the potential side effects from her surgery. The sad part about having an emergency procedure is we may never get the opportunity to tell our loved ones we love them. Will she come out of surgery the same or come out a new person? The procedure involved cutting an incision over the temple of my mother's head from one ear to the other, then remove the brain, put a replacement bone in, place the brain back in the brain cavity and pray. The side effects included excessive memory loss, and losing the ability to read, write, talk, walk, and see. When the brain is removed from the skull, most doctors' state, the recovery is truly dependent on the strength and will of the patient. My mother had the passion to face the fear of surgery.

We all prayed for her wellbeing but it felt as if she was stronger than us and we were the weak links in the family. The head of the family is technically the King but there is something about the Queens of the world. They encompass this web of strength, passion and energy to sustain the bond of the family. The mothers in the world are the veins of the family transferring all of their love and energy throughout the family. Passion kept my dad at the hospital every day and night, not sleeping, working or even blinking because he was focused on a goal.

POST-SURGERY

We waited and waited and then she came out. I would have called her my mother but I did not recognize her face from all the swelling. When the brain is lifted out of the skull the pressure results in massive swelling in the face. My mother could not see, eat or talk. It was a very humbling experience to wake up with a healthy mother and a few hours later see her lying on a hospital bed not talking. The doctor mentioned to us the surgery went well and my mother was very strong, but he could not assure what would happen next. Her recovery would be determined by what's inside of her - her faith and purpose.

In previous situations, the patients learned how to walk, talk and eat within two years and memory is sometimes never regained. But the doctor was confident my mother would make a full recovery based on his personal knowledge of my mother and being her friend.

ROAD TO RECOVERY

The road to recovery begins in the hospital with old pictures from our younger days so my mom could remember our names and ages. During these sessions, I realized my mom lost her memory but did not lose her fight. She had the eye of the tiger; she was fighting to regain her health and memory. The physical and occupational therapist would work her through a few exercises and if she failed, she would beg to do it again, even if it hurt. Her passion to heal from her surgery made me question and focus on the life I was living at the time. I would see her go through good and bad days, but she never gave up, never canceled a therapy session and eventually trained herself to exercise after the therapist departed for the evening. She reminded me of Kevin Durant as a kid, when he stayed in the gym to practice shooting his jump shot over and over again, sometimes spending the night at the local recreational facility just to put up more jumpers. My mother was doing the same thing, but her jump shots were learning how to walk and talk. We began talking to her daily, reminding her of her name and ours. We placed family photos around the room and placed her favorite fragrance in the air as well. We wanted to create a familiar place for her and had the faith she would return to the Queen she was before the surgery. She would glare at us every day, sometimes knowing who we were and others calling for the nurse to remove us from the room because she did not know us.

My mother slowly but surely regained her strength, and began her therapy sessions working harder than ever. The family united during her surgery to create a circle of love to help my mother recover from her surgery and help us get through the tough times. She made a quick and stunning turnaround and regained all of her memory within a month. She began walking on her own within three months and went back to work within eight months.

My mother refused to lie down and take the cards life had handed her. She had been knocked down, but managed to get up with more energy and faith. Life will force us into a corner and we are faced with life or death situations. During this time, we will find out who our real friends are, who the strong are and who the weak people are. After my mother's ordeal, I decided to change some of the friends I was hanging around and re-evaluated my life and the direction I was headed. I changed my circle of friends. I began to travel the world and push myself to the limit. I never could imagine starting my own nonprofit to help kids in lower income areas within inner city get the opportunity to go to college. Her passion changed the purpose for my life and led to the book you are reading.

COACHING/MENTORING

All my life I have been around sports, I have played, watched, coached and trained various sports activities since I was eight years old. I remember chasing Shawn Springs (former Redskin) and teasing Julian Peterson (former 49er and Seattle Seahawk) when playing basketball in summer leagues or AAU basketball. In my community, sports is a big platform for kids to express themselves, mature and generate generational wealth for the family if lucky enough. The ability to share my life experiences with kids who shared the same dreams and goals I had as a kid is priceless. Growing up, I was coached by my dad who still coaches today.

Coaching kids is awesome and then to see them grow into productive citizens was icing on the cake. A coach is more than just a coach; he is a friend, family member, mentor, brother, uncle, taxicab driver, personal trainer, psychologist, financial advisor and many more roles that I know I missed. The coach is everything and the only thing to some kids and their families. Coaching takes a lot of passion and consistency.

To win the love of your players we have to be trustworthy, truthful and honest. If not, teenagers will see right through our intentions and not buy into our authority. Sincerity is very big with young men and women because they witness fakeness every day. A coach with passion is more likeable by his players and staff versus a coach just doing it for the money. Coaching is an opportunity to teach lifelong skills to future leaders within our community. This journey with the kids gave me a wealth of joy, fulfillment and purpose.

The interaction with our future leaders gave me a better understanding of how young men and women think, how times have changed, and how to prepare my daughter for the trials ahead of her. I have gained lifelong friendships with not only the kids, but also their parents and family members. See when we follow our passion we often get more than we can chew in return.

There is a price to driving Justin Alston **(Boston University)** and Matthew McIntosh **(Chicago University)** to the mall and teaching them about college life and how it's different from high school. Both of these young men have proven to be excellent mentees, putting in long hours in the gym and classroom to become productive student athletes and citizens. Watching them grow and mature each year was similar to a father watching their son.

My nephew now a senior in high school was just asking me

to take him running and weight training, now he is stronger than me and signed to a four year scholarship to George Mason University. Leading will keep us hungry, humble and fulfilled.

In graduate school, I was not involved in coaching youth sports for a while, but my brother built up his summer professional basketball leagues with the like of past, current and future NBA players, local talented high school and collegiate players and players from overseas. It is a great program to keep kids off the streets.

My brother called me to coach his All-Stars versus another all-star teams. At first I was like, "Heck no, we will get killed," but then he reaffirmed the team I was coaching was special and they included several future collegiate and NBA stars. It was the first time meeting these young stars and actually seeing what passion and potential was all about. I was blessed to coach them for free; I would have never had the opportunity to meet each one of them. When I go to local NBA games now, all of the players are happy to see me and I am happy to see them following their dreams and living with passion.

SELF-DISCOVERY

The moment of searching for passion and finding it is when we find ourselves. I discovered myself during a conversation amongst friends at an NBA basketball game. I was single at the time, in my late 20's, new house, new car, no kids, and somewhat successful. However, God had a deeper purpose for my life. Week's prior to the game, a friend from South Africa mentioned the cultural, wild life, and social experience in Africa. I was intrigued but was focusing my attention on going to Brazil or Chile. I wanted to learn more and see what Africa was all about. Yes, I wanted to learn more about Africa but it was not top on my to do list, that is until this discussion.

"Every tomorrow has two handles. We can take hold of it with the handle of anxiety or the handle of faith."
-**Henry ward Beecher**

Growing up I always had a fascination for learning new things and "testing the waters. When we are young we think we know it all, but the older we get the more we realize we did not even know the half of it. I grew up thinking Africa was a big jungle, desert and home to great wild life. Unbeknownst to me would I discover Africa is a place of business, building structures, beautifully designed buildings, sophisticated army and place full of opportunity investment for foreigners. Television (T.V.) in U.S. does a great job of showing the half-truth of Africa focusing the majority of the coverage on animals in Africa.

The major difference is the opportunities within the borders of the US are limitless versus the opportunities in Africa are limited for the average African. I get a warm feeling when I travel to Africa; the trips give me an opportunity to learn new things, cultures, people and beliefs. Speaking with the international community while abroad regarding the programs established to provide food, shelter, information and security. Seeing these programs made we want to do more for the youth in the country I was visiting and the youth from which I came from. Seeing people survive off of the bare minimum or less made me think of the material things I complained about in my life. I got a sense of respect sleeping on the floor or Nazareth, Ethiopia with family and praying to God for the blessings. It's a very humbling experience to see men fighting in the streets of Barbados with machetes and rocks, aiming to not only harm but to dismember or to kill. We have to always remember when we are suffering someone is suffering a little bit more and it can get worse.

Prior to leaving for Africa I had an interesting discussion with two colleagues of mine, one was happy and the other thought

I was crazy and suggested I submit myself for mental evaluation. I thought to myself really? It must be the wine. He then said, "Why would you go over there where there are only lions and tigers?" I shook my head and just continued listening to him, "I like my water hot and my cable channels." As I listened to this articulate and educated individual speak on an elementary level education of Africa, I understood everything is not for everybody and I could not displace my wants and needs on my friends. They were entitled to their opinion.

Sometimes we seek validation from our friends and family, instead of just trusting our gut feelings. My gut led me to write this book and visit places in the world I dreamed of as a kid. When we go searching for our passion we often find our true selves, which is forever changing as we grow. But once we figure out who we really are, we can begin to search for the things we love to do.

Similar to the having the opportunity to coach future NBA stars, situations like this and traveling the world rarely happen and we often fall behind our fears and don't chase our curiosity. Well, call me "Curious George". If it sparks my interest and intellect, it's worth the risk for me. Think of all the stereotypes in the world we listen too, which prevent us from thinking outside the box. Release perceptions and assumptions and live with the reality or better yet take my approach. If you want to find out how the people are in China, go there or talk to someone who has been there. America has given me a strong foundation, now it's my turn to return the favor and bring something back to America to educate and teach others to follow their dreams.

ACCEPTANCE

This section is dedicated to two young ladies who have taken the guts, passion and self-love to share their HIV positive status with the world and they are still standing strong within their community as HIV ambassadors. HIV- related stigma and discrimination persist as major obstacles to an effective HIV response in all parts of the world. Numerous studies have linked HIV-related stigma with delayed HIV testing, non-disclosure to partners and poor engagement with HIV services.

People who experience stigma and discrimination report a range of negative effects, including loss of income, isolation from communities and inability to participate as a productive member of society as a result of their HIV status. But these two high profile young ladies, one a successful actor and another a radio personality, choose to not only share their status but remain in the lime light and keep pushing forward.

I remember working for a HIV clinical trials group and having a conversation with an investigator of the international program. She disclosed information on a case where a husband contracted HIV and infected his wife. He did not disclose his activity outside of the house and when he realized he contracted HIV he did not disclose this information. This prompted the question, "Are we ever safe?" She responded, "No". In today's society when a couple argues they leave the relationship and instead of being mad and isolated to himself or herself, we tend to gravitate to someone else. This leads to bad things happening because we are acting out of impulsive anger. I know many married couples and I could imagine the wife coming home and asking the husband to wear a condom, his first thought would be why, and then are you sleeping with someone else? Married couples rarely use condoms, unless they are trying to prevent a baby, but there are alternative birth control methods. It made me think of how safe we are today, if our partners are not openly honest about their wrongdoings.

In today's society a lie could kill us. We could set up a 24-hour surveillance operation to monitor our spouses every move but then we kill the trust in the relationship, which is the foundation. Thinking back in college the health care professionals would recommend students get tested every six months, but in today's society it seems even married couples need to have annually or biannually HIV-test dates. But the problem is not solely on marriages; it's all relationships.

Think about the HIV of David Lee Mangum from Missouri who has known his HIV positive status for ten years and purposefully infected over three hundred women over a ten-year period. Then the story of the pastor in Atlanta who was convicted for intentionally having sex with two women and not disclosing his HIV positive status, telling the women, "I did not tell you because God did not want me to".

Next, consider the story of the young lady who was infected by her fiancée and only found out during her pregnancy exam. It takes a sick person to infect the person they love enough to marry and bare children, to hide their bisexual tendencies and their HIV positive status only to reveal it after a pregnancy exam. It seems the pregnancy period is where most people find out, they are HIV positive instead of getting randomly tested.

We need to pay attention to the people we choose to get into relationships with and not rush the courting process. One of the worst cases I discovered was the case in Florida, on Keith 'Keyoko' Sumlin, 21 years old who knowingly infected a 15-year-old boy, recorded the events, posted it on Facebook and bragged about it. **There is not a jail cell in the world dirty enough to place this type of person in.**

In a world full of people hiding their true identity and weaknesses, it gives me pleasure to see people like Magic Johnson, and the two women included below who are on top of the world and still have the courage, fortitude and self-love to admit their HIV positive status. We are all human and we all make mistake, but don't compound a mistake or take your frustrations out on others because you feel someone purposefully did something to infect you.

"Though the night is dark and gloomy the sun will rise and bring a brighter day."
-Onie Bell Hill

Meet **Criselda Kananda** and **Lesego Motsepe** (deceased 2014) two beautiful women who have given their lives to fight HIV. Both are respectable and well-known leaders in their community and have been spoken out about how to prevent others from making the same mistake. Ms. Kananda has produced a Positive Talk CD with the intentions of inspiring others to take responsibility for their lives, find purpose and passion in living.

When life hits us with a tornado and blows our house off the hinges and all is lost. We need to muster the energy and faith to move forward and build a stronger foundation. The lesson learned from the previous storm will help us for the future storm coming our way. The late Ms. Lesego Motsepe is a well-known actress in South African soap opera television shows. Mrs. Motsepe was a HIV ambassador who became infected by the virus and on world AIDS day disclosed her positive status in effort to be a bridge of hope for those living with HIV. We need more people to stand up and be accountable for their actions.

The key to fixing a mistake is not to compound the mistake with a bigger mistake. In a world lacking transparency, it takes a passionate person full of life to disclose their HIV status. It takes guts and strength to keep going after the world has knocked us down and I commend everyone in the world who has faced their fears, and stood up for their beliefs. If a person truly loves themselves they will disclose their status to the person they love and give them the courtesy to decide their future

Message from this chapter: *The ultimate measure of success is being able to live with your mistakes and help others prevent the same mistakes. The most valuable gift in the world is given someone else, who doesn't have the chances you have, the opportunity to succeed.*

SHARE YOUR STORY

As your reading comes to an end, life will continue and I would like to hear more about you on my website and how this book or any of my other books have sparked something within you. The point of collecting your point of testimony or stories is to spread the positive energy to others. If you would like to share your store, please visit www.passionwith-in.com. I will showcase stories periodically via my Facebook page (www.facebook.com/ohtestimony), my website and Twitter page (www.twitter.com/HILLMBA).

In addition, you may want to check out the *Passion With-in Workbook*, which is an interactive book to help you mental work on developing the passion within yourself today.

GO SHARE YOUR STORY TODAY!

ACKNOWLEDGEMENT

Special thanks goes out to my late grandfather Russell Floyd (Atlanta) and grandmother Onie Bell Hill (Greenwood, SC) who had the courage and strength to setup a family and raise them with morals and values regardless of the chaotic world around them.

The importance of grandparents and their wisdom has been a blessing in my life and I work to instill the same interaction with my daughter and my mother. Still living and the strength of my family is the great Corrine Floyd, currently residing in Atlanta at the tender age of 25 years old (she is always 25), she serves as the prime example of why I choose to help and uplift others and never make excuses.. My grandparents subliminally gave me the ingredients to success before I was ready to accept them at a young age. I am forever in debt to their hard work and continuous love. There isn't a word in the dictionary that can convey the way I feel about each of my grandparents, but they know I love them with my soul.

I would like to acknowledge my family for always believing in my ability and investing their love within me daily, for without them I would not be. The amount of time, dedication and solidarity involved with writing a book can become, at times, a bit selfish and unwanted. Sometimes missing family celebrations and outgoing to continue the urge to write my thoughts. However, throughout my writing experience my family has motivated the entire time to keep going and finish the task. For them, I forever grateful.

Special thanks goes out to my mother and father, whom have been my best friends since I came out the womb. The first signs of love are usually from your mother and father and these two individuals superseded expectations. Even when I deserved a switch kick in the rear-end my mother and father managed to end it with love and clarification. For their continuous support and inspirational words that I can do anything I ever wanted to will always remain saturated in my heart. I did not choose my parents, but I am blessed to have two strong and committed parents who understand the importance of living a good life, helping others and leaving the world a better place.

Special thanks goes out to GOD for giving me the wisdom, favor and Holy Spirit to finish the task I started. Sometimes I don't know why he choose me to write and speak a certain message, but I will never doubt his word, decision or purpose for my life. I am not a perfect person, but I work to be a better person every day through continuous positive actions and prayer.

I also would like to take the time out to thank the reader for supporting my writing because without your support I realize I can't reach success. I see your purchase as a partnership and I plan on keeping my end of the agreement. I will continue to motivate and inspire the world with positive messages.

ABOUT THE AUTHOR

PRODUCT OF PRINCE GEORGES COUNTY, MD AND A STRONG FAMILY!

Oumar Hill is an entrepreneur, passionprenuer, motivational speaker, author, and coach who has touched the lives of many people all around the world with his passion and purpose to serve others. He is the founder of TEAM FINESSE and O Hill & Associates, which are organization-serving people in Washington DC, Virginia, Maryland, Ethiopia, South Africa and Caribbean Islands. Team Finesse places intensive focuses on development through leadership development, teamwork, good sportsmanship and high emphasis on reliability training. Mr. Hill holds an MBA in Global Business and dedicated his life to being a catalyst for change and a voice for generations. Mr. Hill has continued with his commitment to serving others and in helping them in meet challenges successfully. To learn more about Mr. Hill read his blog at www.passionwith-in.com. Follow him on Facebook at facebook.com/ohtestimony. Follow him on Tweeter at Tweeter/HILLMBA & Twitter/Passionprenuer

❖❖❖❖❖❖❖❖❖

LOVE AND LIGHT IN YOUR LIFE!

NOTES

INTRODUCTION
1. Prayers of comfort & Hope-Holding on to Faith, 2013, pg. 44.
2. *Prayers of comfort & Hope-Holding on to faith, 2013, pg. 31.*
3. Simple Truths for Creating Happiness + Success: Emotional Equations, 2012, pg. 3 & 185.

DIG DEEPER
1. Bial, S. (2012, May 8). Five Steps to Finding Your Passion. Retrieved from http://www.psychologytoday.com/blog/prescriptions-life/201205/five-steps-finding-your-passion.

FIND IT WITH-IN
1. Rizzo, P. (2012, January 16). 5 Health Benefits of List Making. Retrieved from http://www.listproducer.com/2012/01/16/5-health-benefits-of-list-making/.
2. Scott, E. (2012, October 11). The Difference Between Optimists and Pessimist. Retrieved from thttp://stress.about.com/od/optimismspirituality/a/optimism benefit_2.htm.
3. Ten professional development benefits of volunteering by Mary, v Merrill, LSW, Merrill associates.
4. *Prayers of comfort & Hope-Holding on to faith, 2013, pg. 39.*
5. Arina's SELF HELP BLOG (2011, January 11). Tag Archives: overcoming fears. Retrieved from http://www.arinanikitina.com/tag/overcoming-fears,

MAXIMIZING PASSION
1. Prayers of comfort & Hope-Holding on to faith, 2013, pg. 355.

2. Prayers of comfort & Hope-Holding on to faith, 2013, pg. 280.

KEY FACTORS WITH-IN YOU
1. WALE-AMBITION lyrics. Retrieved from https://play.google.com/music/preview/Toir2wyx7ildjzxv3zsy563fi7a?lyrics=1&utm_source=google&utm_medium=search&utm_campaign=lyrics
2. Prayers of comfort & Hope-Holding on to faith, 2013, pg. 127.

PASSIONPRENUERS
1. *Prayers of comfort & Hope-Holding on to faith, 2013, pg. 224.*
2. Passion and Purpose (Coleman, Gulati &Segovia) page 1
3. Jacques, R. 16 wildly successful people who overcame hug obstacles to get there (2013, September 25). Retrieved from http://www.huffingtonpost.com/2013/09/25/successful-people-obstacles_n_3964459.html

BE COMPASSIONATE
1. *Prayers of comfort & Hope-Holding on to faith, 2013, pg. 39.*
2. Casruso, G. He lost 275 pounds, reunited with love (2014, February 17). Retrieved from http://www.cnn.com/2014/02/17/health/weight-loss-lee-jordan/

MENTAL HEALTH
1. Cherry, K.. What Is Self-Actualization? (2011, February). Retrieved from http://psychology.about.com/od/theoriesofpersonality/a/hierarchyneeds_2.htm
2. Maslow, A. H. (1943). A Theory of Human Motivation, *Psychological Review 50*, 370-96.
3. The Ideal of Self-Fulfillment. Retrieved from http://press.princeton.edu/chapters/s6413.pdf

4. Daniel Yankelovich, New Rules: Searching for Self-Fulfillment in a World Turned Upside Down (New York: Random House, 1981).
5. Henry Sidgwick, The Ethics of T. H. Green, Herbert Spencer, and J. Martineau (London: Macmillan, 1902), p. 64; Sidgwick, The Methods of Ethics, 7th ed. (London: Macmillan, 1907), pp. 91, 95.

AUTHOR'S TESTIMONY
1. *Prayers of comfort & Hope-Holding on to faith, 2013, pg. 58*
2. Global Report UNAIDS report on the global AIDS EPIDEMEIC 2013 (www.unaids.org), (United Nations Global Report page 84)
3. *Prayers of comfort & Hope-Holding on to faith, 2013, pg. 85*

www.ingramcontent.com/pod-product-compliance
Lightning Source LLC
Chambersburg PA
CBHW070145100426
42743CB00013B/2819